Ruth Amster
Artist

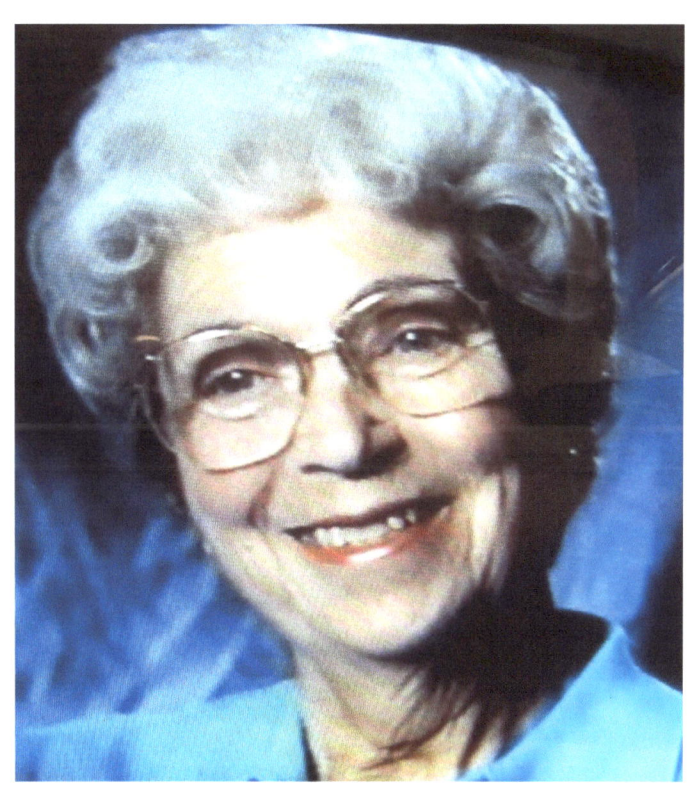

Edited by
Vivian Chepourkoff Hayes, MA, MS

Copyright 2017

AUTHOR'S NOTE: I met Ruth at her studio, which was all windows, with a ceiling two stories high. That was the only time I had a chance to photograph her art. Unfortunately some pictures had glass on them, and had reflections which blocked the image. Others were hung very high, distorting the shape of the painting.

Her story was recorded on a videotape. There was also a UTube video comparing her paintings with her husband Dolph's photography, which is used in this book. I give credit to the people who made these videos. I am the editor who put this together.

To contact me, my email is vivianhayes154@yahoo.com. My website is vivianchepourkoffhayes.com, and write to P.O. Box 551, Ridgecrest, CA 93555.

I have written many books, available on Amazon under Vivian Chepourkoff Hayes, or Vivian Hayes. I would love to hear from you!

Ruth is Jewish, born and raised in the Bronx, N.Y. After both her parents died, at around age twenty-six, she moved to Washington, D.C. and got a job at the Government Printing Press. She designed brochures or handouts.

Her husband "Dolph" (he did not want to use his real name, Adolf, because of Adolph Hitler) and she moved to Ridgecrest around forty years ago. He photographed as a hobby. They traveled all over, to Russia, to China, anywhere that was interesting. Ruth sketched and Dolph photographed. At first they really didn't like each other's work, but as they traveled and worked together, their work became more alike.

Ruth traveled north on Highway 14 to Owens Lake for two years and painted what she saw. She had a show at the Ridgecrest Maturango Museum in 2003, called "The Many Moods of Owens Lake."

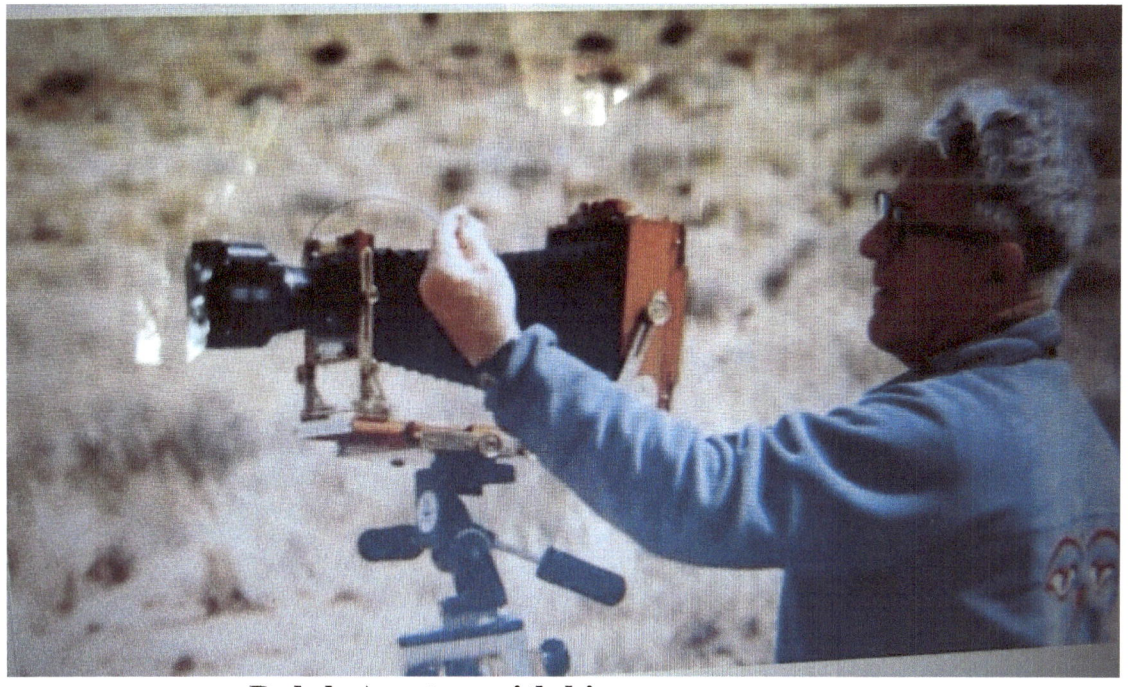

Dolph Amster, with his camera.

At the time of her show, Ruth was interviewed about her ideas and experiences as an artist. Here is that interview.

I was born and raised in New York City at a time which was great. I had a kindergarten teacher who encouraged my mother to take me to museums. I was accepted by the High School of Music and Art.

As I grew a little older, I went by subway to Works Progress Administration (WPA) classes at the High School of Music and Art. It was an experiment by Mayor La Guardia. Anyone could go to that school if they took a test in music or art. I could sing, and was accepted.

During World War II, there were a number of well known artists living in New York. New York became like a little Paris. Matisse, and Archipenko were there. The sculptor Archipenko critiqued a sculpture of mine. I was offered two scholarships for further study, one in music, and one in art. The art scholarship was for Black Mountain College, a famous college for the arts in North Carolina. My mother didn't want me to leave New York.

I dropped the ball in art. I stopped painting and went on to major in art history at the University of Maryland. My minor was studio. I studied with Mark Lewis, a well known abstract expressionist painter.

I organized docent tours at New York's Smithsonian. The experience with the Smithsonian helped me when I came to Ridgecrest. I wasn't painting then but my experience helped me organize docent tours with the Maturango Museum in Ridgecrest. I was the Gallery Director and set up exhibits. When I resigned from the exhibit gallery, I started painting and that's where I'm at now.

Q. WHAT INFLUENCED YOU?

Teachers. Mostly teachers. Kindergarten. Elementary. Mrs. Futterman. Mrs. Fury. From the time I was very little, somehow they would take me to the library and encourage me to sketch. My mother. She took me to the museum. We moved to a new neighborhood. My art made me known and I made friends. There was a time when my mother was ill and I was separated from her.

Q. WHAT MEDIUM DO YOU PREFER?

I have worked in several different mediums. I have found the subject will dictate the medium and what I want to paint. Here in the desert, acrylic is difficult to work with. They dry too fast for me. I work in watercolor and oil. Pastels. I avoided pastels like the plague. I bought a big set of pastels. My friend, Mary Cutsinger, who, of course is an exceptionally fine pastel painter, said, "sell me that set." Finally, last year I started to use it. If I had a preferred medium at the moment, it would be pastels. I don't feel as secure in it yet as the other mediums.

Q. WHAT STYLE DO YOU PREFER?

I've always been attracted to and I painted in an abstract way, but it changed when I moved here. Everything was clearly delineated. The air was so clear. My style did change. I think it is still changing. Some people have a signature style. You know exactly who did the painting. My friend, Joanne, my friend Sue, you know who did it.

Q. HOW DO YOU DECIDE WHAT TO PAINT?

Well, usually, I approach it this way. I'm moved by something, whether it is a flower or a scene. I may take a photograph, or do a quick sketch. Oftentimes then I'll think about it. and start to do little sketches. Somehow composing a painting in my mind is very important to me, so I will do some preliminary sketches. My palette and my composition expresses how I feel.

Sometimes you decide to paint something and it takes a life of its own. It goes in a different direction and you have to decide whether you will go with it. Some very exciting things happen. You have to have enough confidence to go with it. Subject matter. I would say landscapes and still-lifes are very nice. I don't do portraits.

Q. WHY DID YOU GO WITH ART?

I think I've always loved color and shapes and so on. Some people are interested in numbers. I've had a very traditional art education at the high school. In 1941 I saw Picasso's Guernica at the museum. Georgia O'Keefe came to our high school. I was the editor of our paper. I remember being pushed to go up to her and ask questions. Somehow she must have surmised how I felt. She started to interview me.

Q. WHY DO YOU CREATE?

Why does anyone create? We all have a need to create. A child who decides what color he wants to fix up his room, or how to arrange his sox in a drawer is creating. I think life would be unbearable if we couldn't create. I think that is part of our human nature.

The first time you get excited about something, you get to a point that you go to a special place, then you are not sure where do you go from here? You can't seem to communicate how you feel.

Ruth belongs to a group of painters. She said, I think we are an unusual group of women. We have to respect the anonymity. Being part of the group has made me feel like I'm a painter again. Sure, there's a wonderful reward about creation. If you can share, It's like giving someone something special.

I think art and music is what makes life bearable. It gives us structure. The things that are really important to us are those discoveries. If you are a writer, keep a journal. An artist, observe, and sketch. Go to exhibits. Whenever I could, if there was an art club, I would belong.

Mornings I like to watch the sunrise. I like classical music. It's serene. I may just walk around my studio. I find that being in my studio about a half an hour, I'll take a break and have a cup of coffee or just walk around the lot.

Q. WHEN IS A PAINTING FINISHED?

I have some of these paintings around that I've done five or six times and I still haven't gotten what I want. I think there is more angst in painting for me than there might be for others. It's been more than that, learning that we all have the same machinations, the same insecurities. Who am I kidding? I may feel I need to do more, but that painting may go into a show wet.

SOME OBSERVATIONS ON PAINTING AND PHOTOGRAPHY.

You don't see as much as much as the camera sees. You see something small in relationship to what the camera sees. You focus on something that you're interested in. You have to learn to focus in on what you want to say and decide what is the best way of communicating your idea. I think that applies to anybody, to a painter, to a photographer, an architect an when he is designing something.

Why do people take photographs? Do you take it because you want to keep a record of where you went, or someone you met and won't see again and you want to have it? Or you see a beautiful sunset and you want to capture it.

All of those things involve different approaches. If you just want a record of something, it doesn't involve an artistic point of view. You just want to capture it. If you are moved by what you see, and you want capture what moves you, that involves decisions, and that involves using techniques. You need to know the technique you can use to express what you are seeing in order to paint it.

Actually photography today is just another art form. It is just another medium. There are so many things you can do with photographs. You can remove things, you can manipulate it, do things that you couldn't do in earlier times. Once you rely on tools, you are getting into making decisions about what you want.

Dolph and I used to go out together, he with his camera, and me with my paints. As you all know, it doesn't take as long to take a picture than to do a painting. It got so we would try to do the same thing in our own way, in our own medium. It's interesting to see how he tackled the subject in comparison to painting scenery.

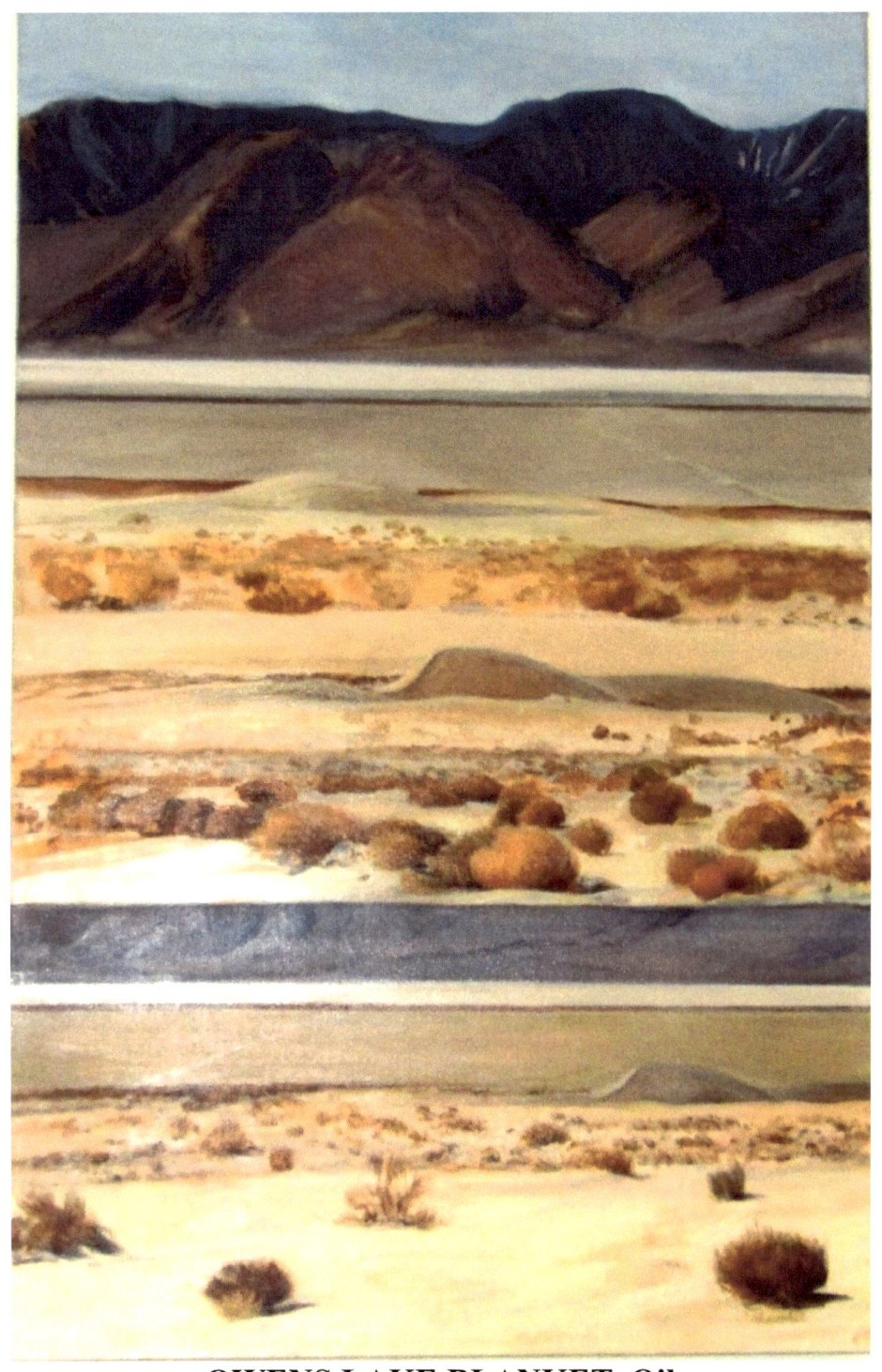

OWENS LAKE BLANKET. Oil.

In preparation for my show at Maturango Museum, "The Many Moods of Owen's Lake," I had got together many photographs that I had taken. I spent almost a year and a half going to the lake. I wanted to capture what I thought of as the essence of Owens Lake.

One day I sat down with a whole bunch of photographs. There were many of these photographs. You know, maybe I can do a collage of these photographs. I wanted one picture and I wanted it to say something. I wanted it to say Owen's Lake. I was playing with these photographs. I had something that looked like a blanket.

I cropped these photographs into a pattern. This is my Owens Lake Blanket. I had people who were confused by this blanket. They weren't sure where the mountains were and where the desert ended. It was like doing a warp in a carpet. Photography played an important part in forming this painting.

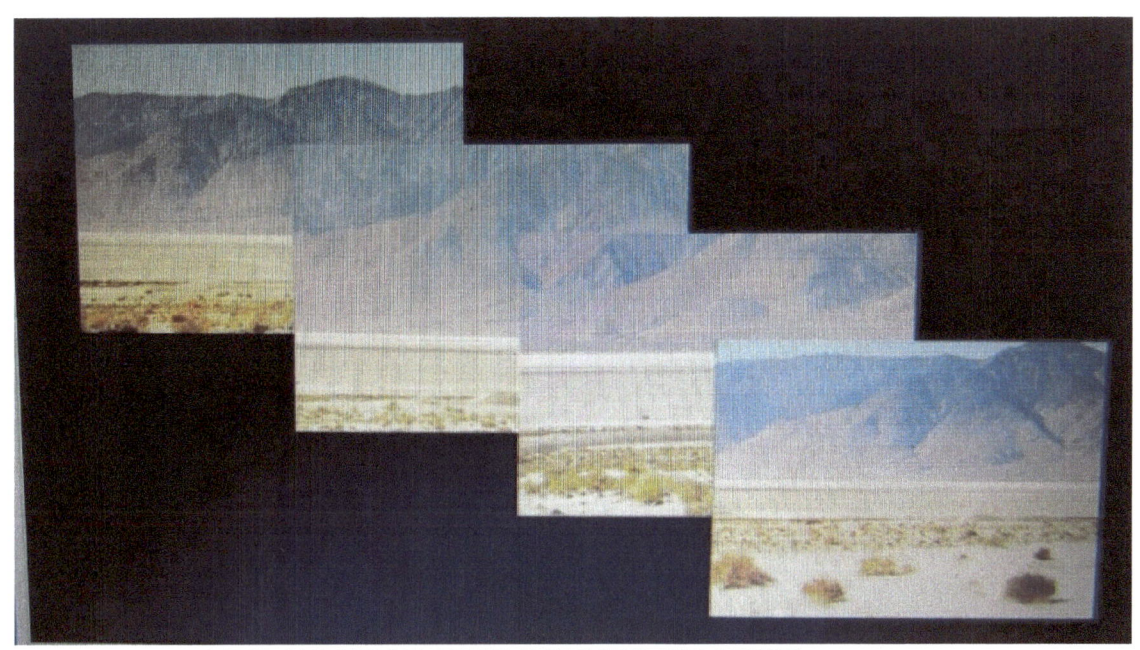

ARRANGING THE PHOTOGRAPHS.

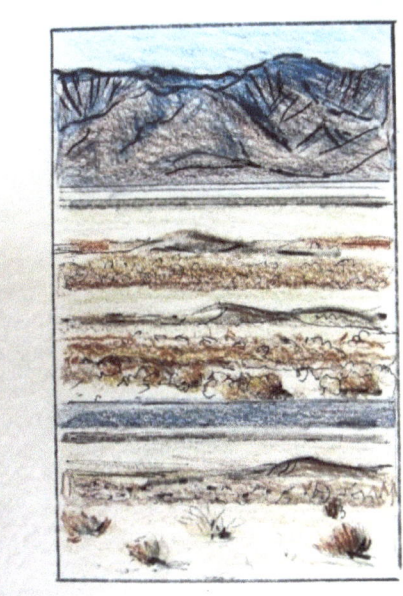

A SKETCH IN PREPARATION FOR THE PAINTING.

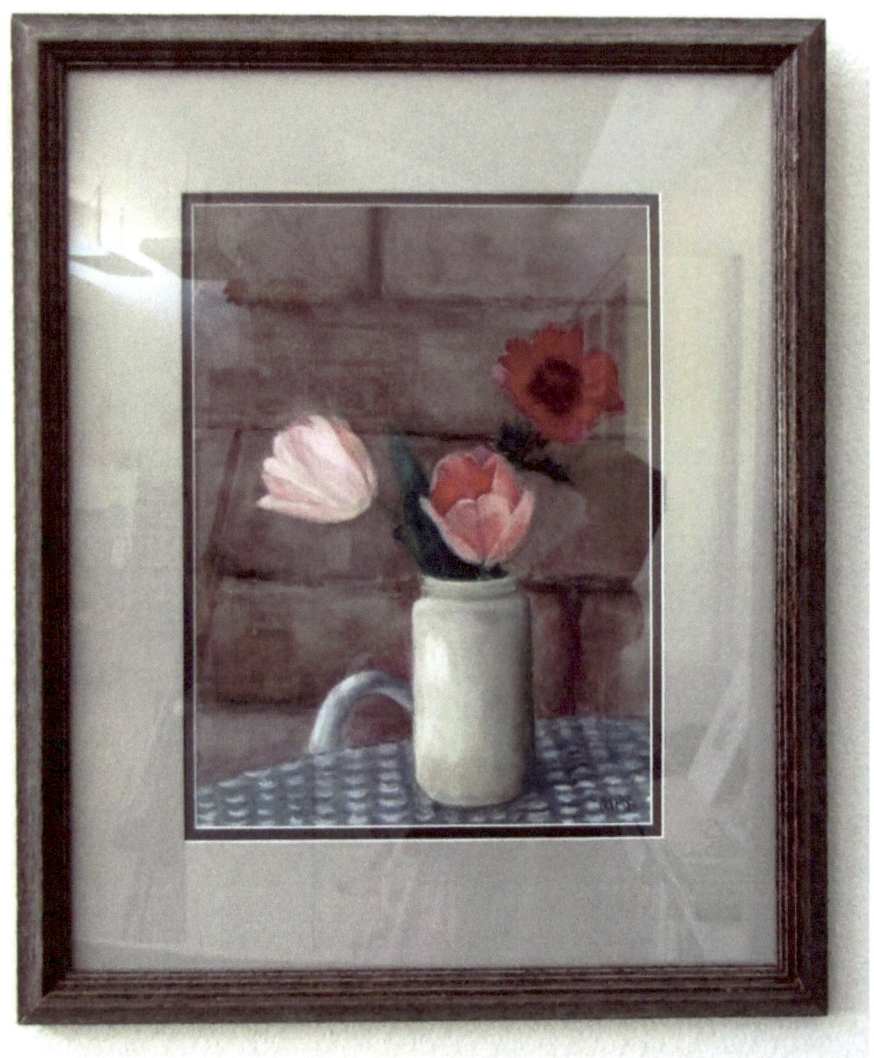

SPRING FLOWERS. Watercolor.
    I fell in love with these tulips. I felt happy when I picked the colors, especially the pink. I brought them inside the house and found this little jug to put them in. The stone wall blended with the flowers and kept the mood. When I am not traveling, I like to do still-lifes.

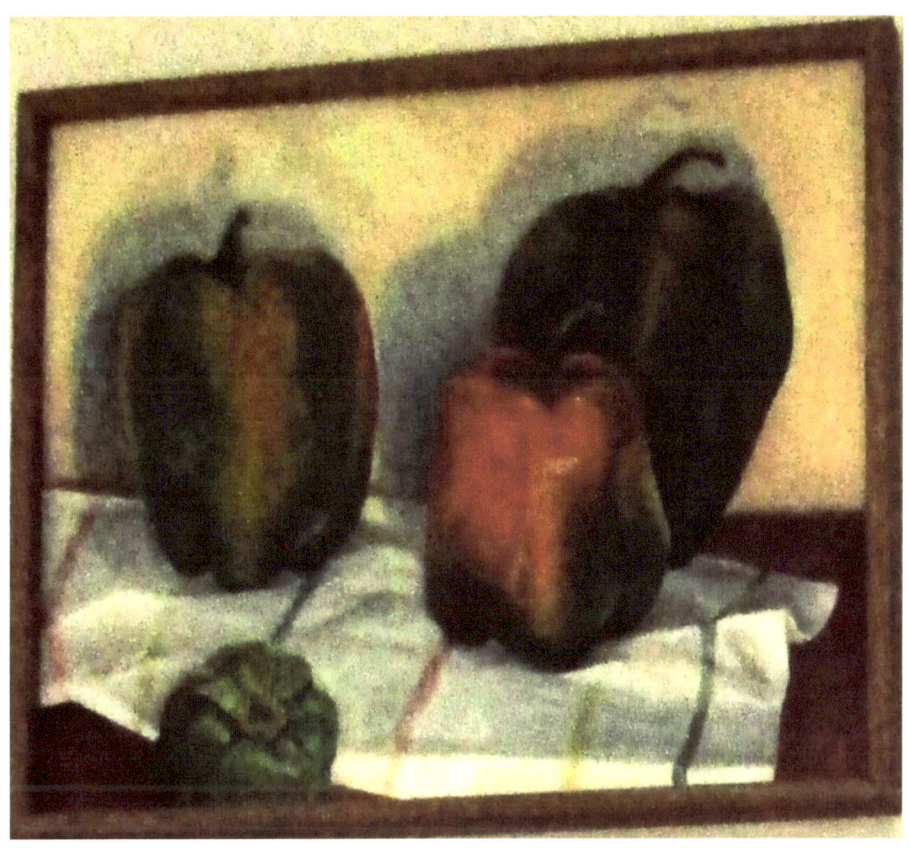

PEPPERS. Oil.

The arrangement of peppers makes an abstract shape, with the small pepper going off the edge on purpose, to anchor the forms to the picture.

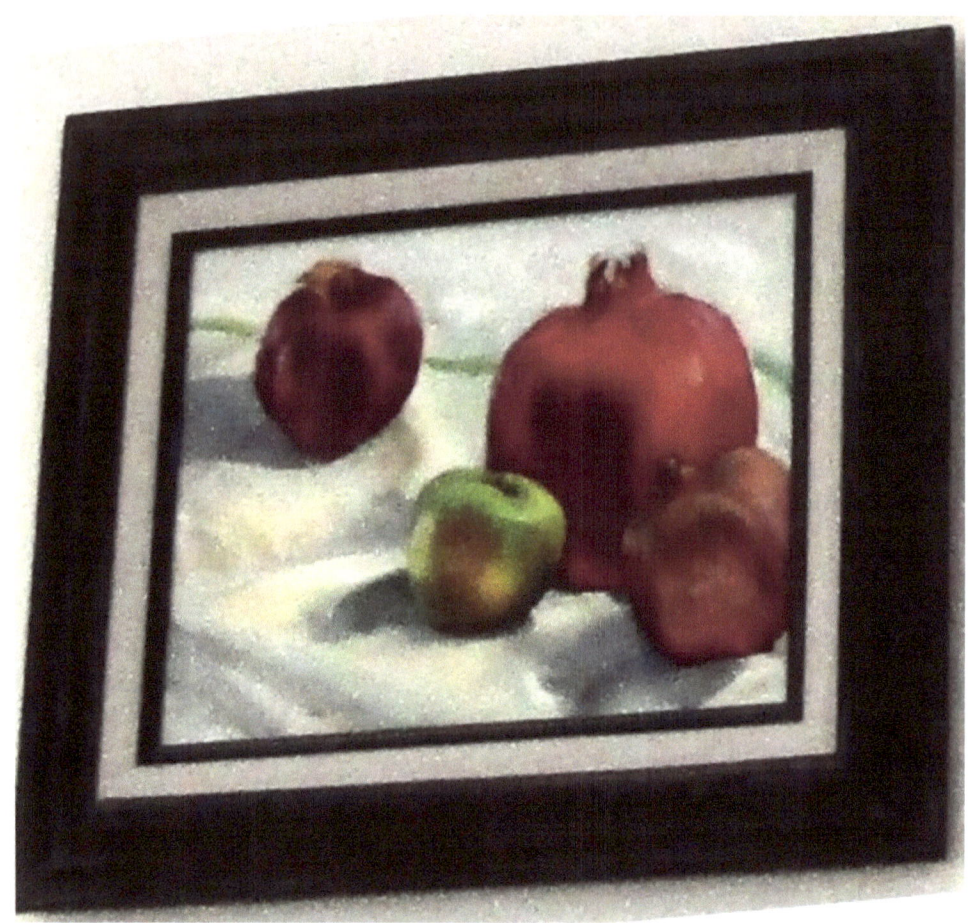

POMEGRANATES WITH AN APPLE. Oil.

Again, this painting is a contrast of shapes with the green apple a contrast of color against the red pomegranates. I did this exercise at Cerro Coso College.

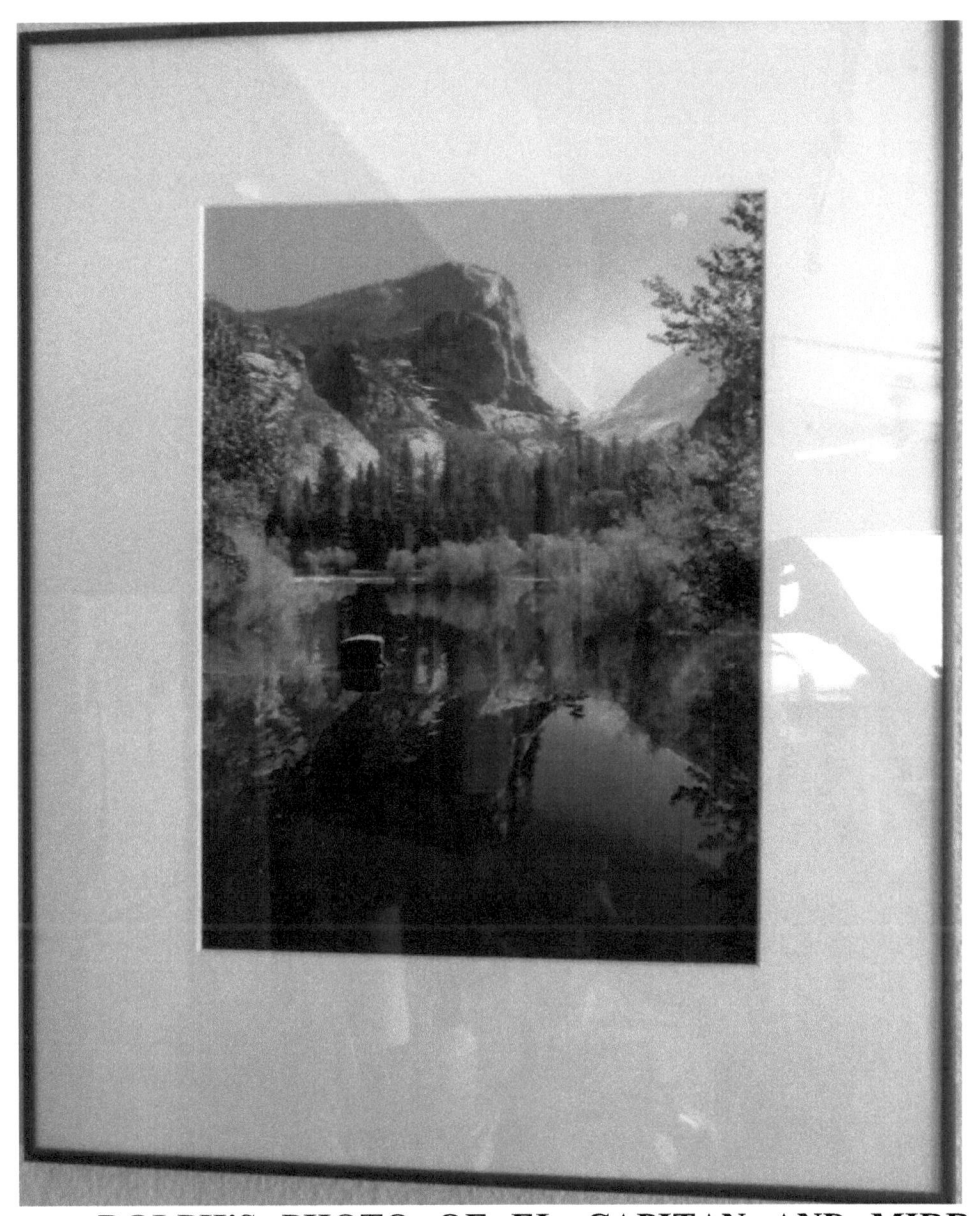

DOLPH'S PHOTO OF EL CAPITAN AND MIRROR LAKE IN YOSEMITE NATIONAL PARK.

El Capitan is one of the famous formations at Yosemite. Dolph's photo captures the reflection in the well named "Mirror Lake."

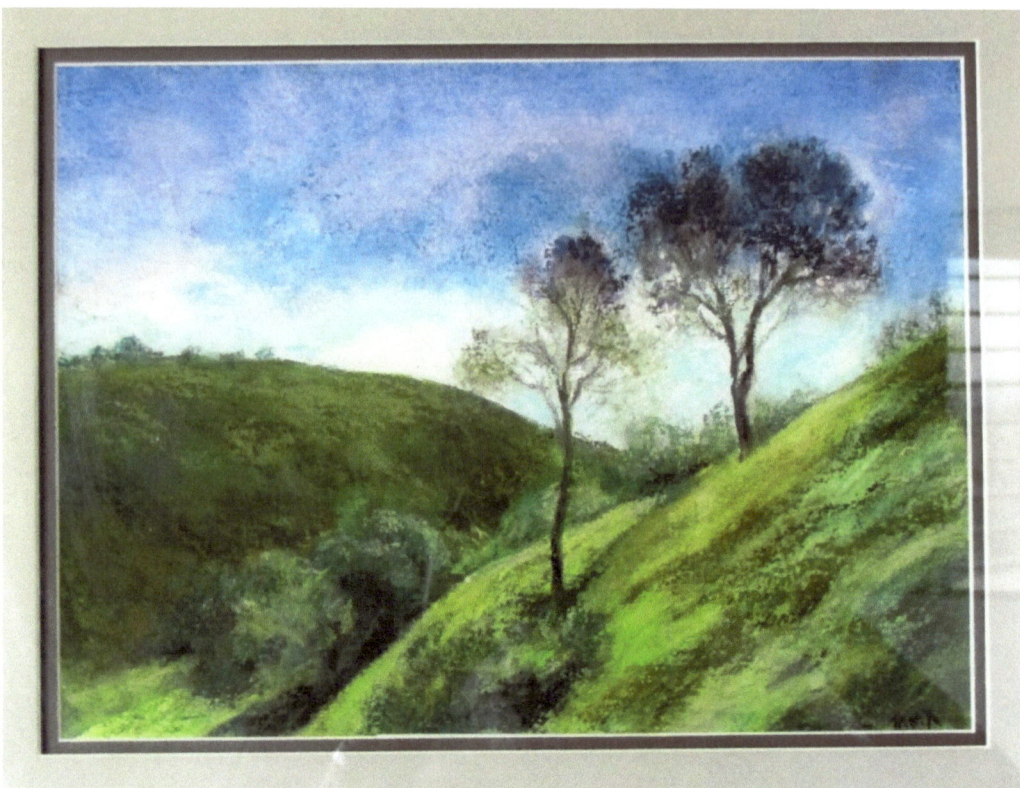

CALIFORNIA HILLS IN THE SPRING. Watercolor.

This scene was facing a river. There weren't many trees on the hills. These two lonely trees were so lovely in contrast to the hills, I just had to capture it.

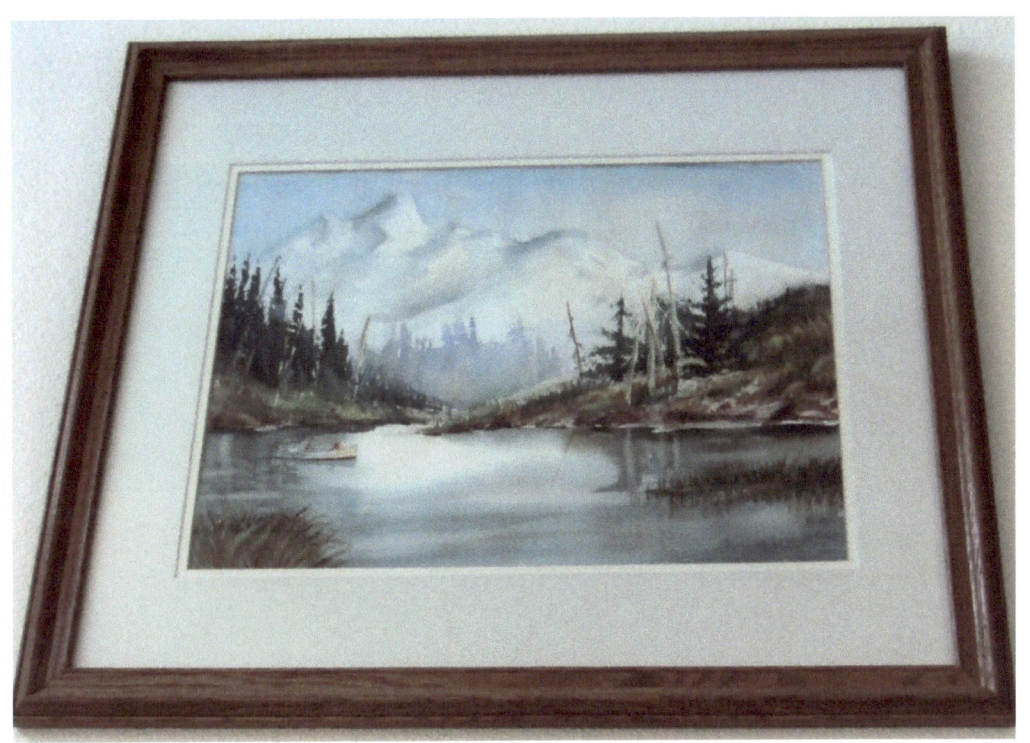

MOUNTAINS AFTER A STORM. Watercolor.
Sierra mountains in California.

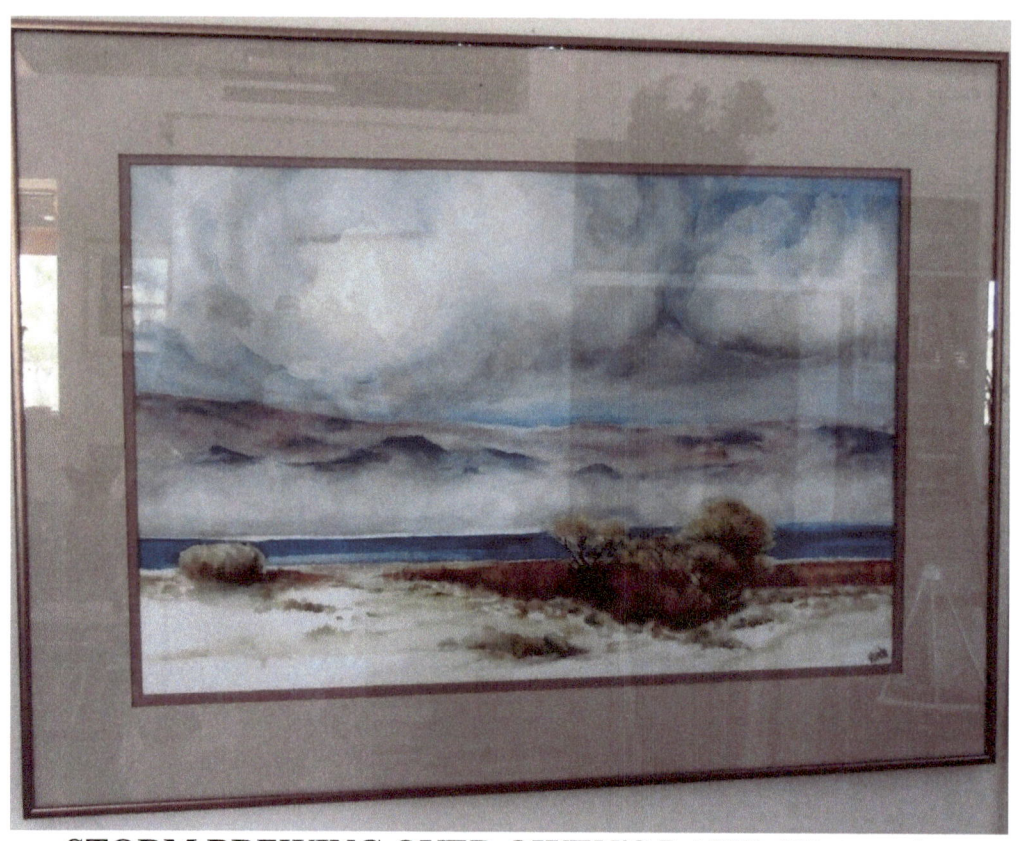

STORM BREWING OVER OWEN'S LAKE. Watercolor.
This shows an ominous atmosphere.

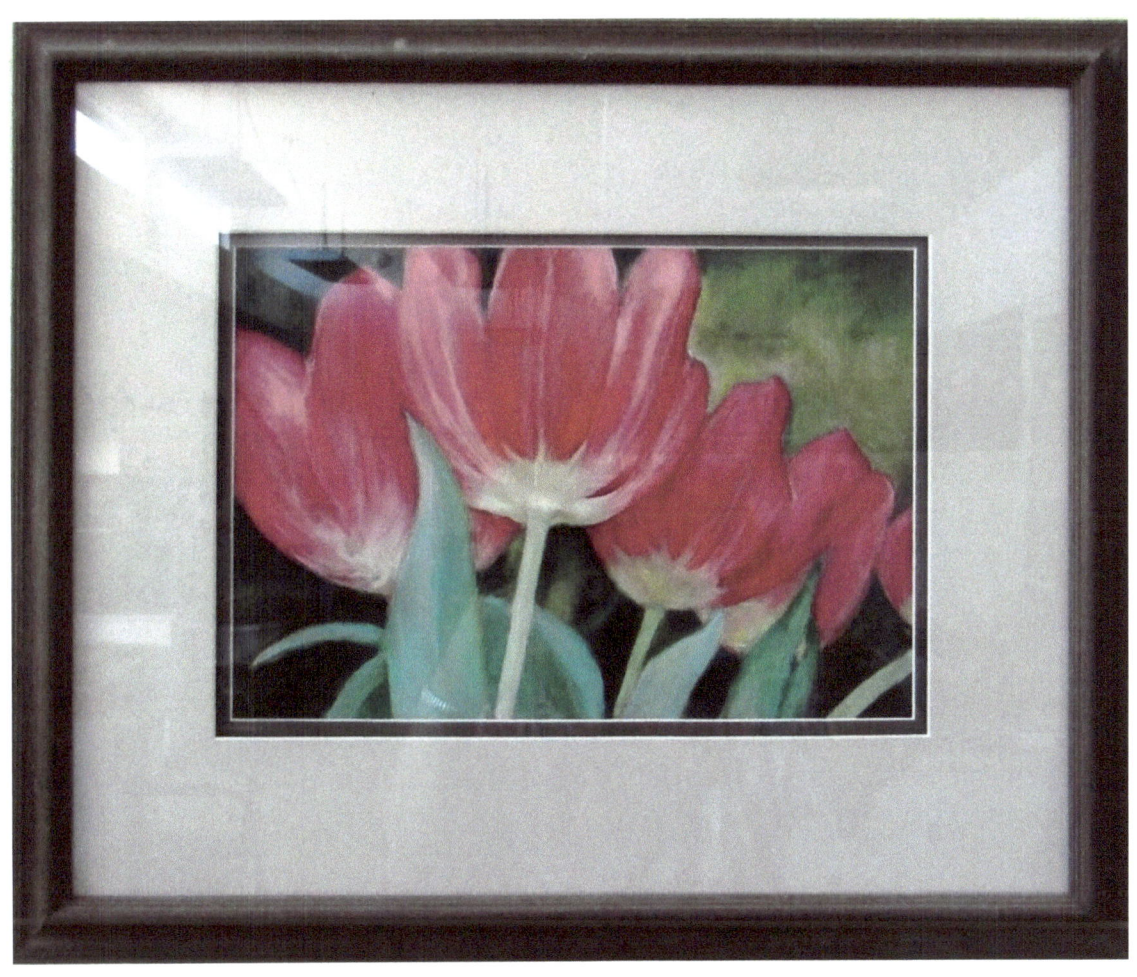

TULIPS. Watercolor.
The shapes make an abstract design like a ballet. A dance of the flowers.

RUTH AND DOLPH TOOK TRIPS WHICH INSPIRED THEIR WORK.

RHYOLITE, NEVADA

I love Rhyolite. Dolph and I have gone up to it many times. I'm sorry to say it has kind of disintegrated. It's kind of sad in a way. We don't exactly paint the same things. We were drawn to different views. I didn't see as much of the drama as he did. Dolph is so good when it comes to something dramatic.

I think my painting is more of a record of a place. He waited for the right lighting. My painting to me is more of a record. I was fascinated with the environment. I didn't see the drama. I saw the drabness that the desert can often appear to be. That's what I saw more. I saw something that was dead. Dolph saw a wonderful mood.

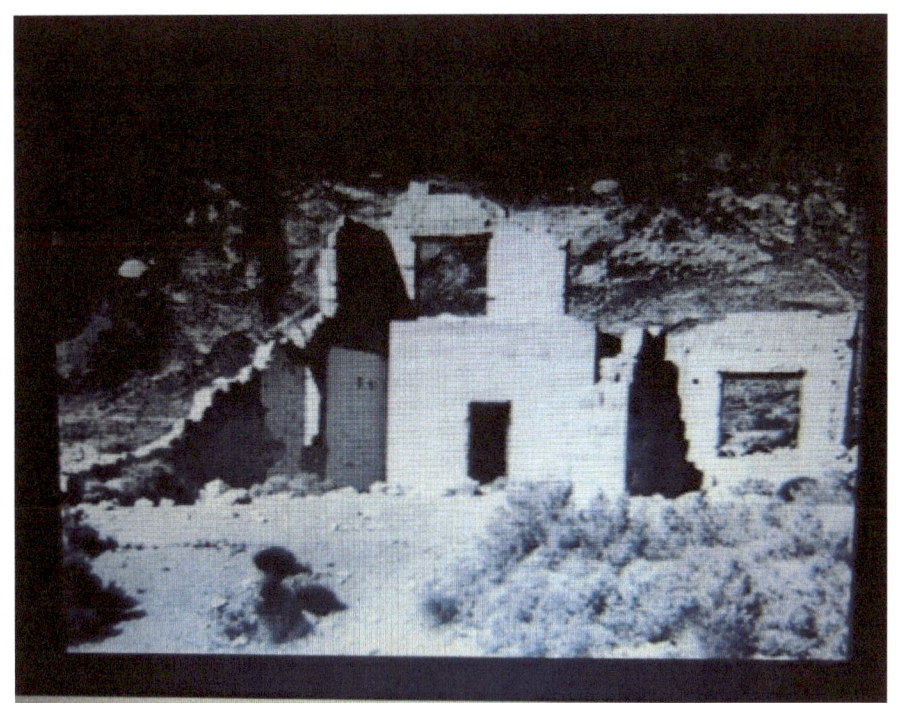

RHYOLITE BY DOLPH. Photograph.

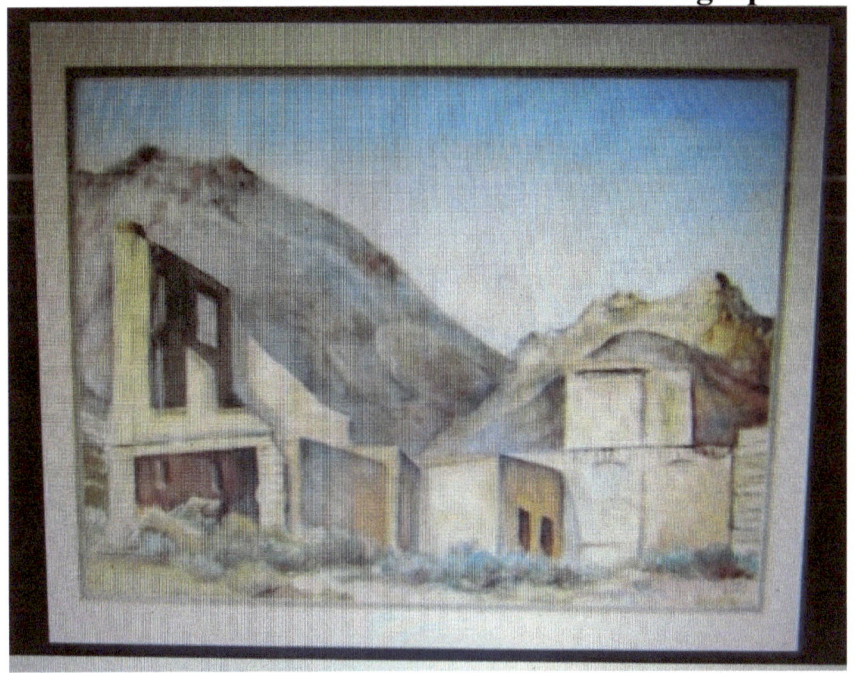

RHYOLITE BY RUTH. Watercolor

ALABAMA HILLS

This is the Alabama Hills. Dolph and I went up there one day. We weren't sure we were going to do the same area. I think Dolph's photograph is beautiful and communicates more of a mood because of how he used his values in conveying a mood than my little sketch does. My sketch is what it is--a sketch. I just sketched what I saw. I didn't have a particular feeling like Dolph did. If I had wanted to do a large painting, a real big painting, I would have made decisions. Did I want to do it later in the afternoon or in the morning? I didn't take into mind how I wanted to see it.

There you are, sometimes you communicate more of a mood in photography than in a sketch. I called my painting a sketch. I was taken by the shapes and some of the little shadows. Dolph's photograph, you can't miss it. Mine looks so light and bright, not so sculptural as Dolph's photograph is.

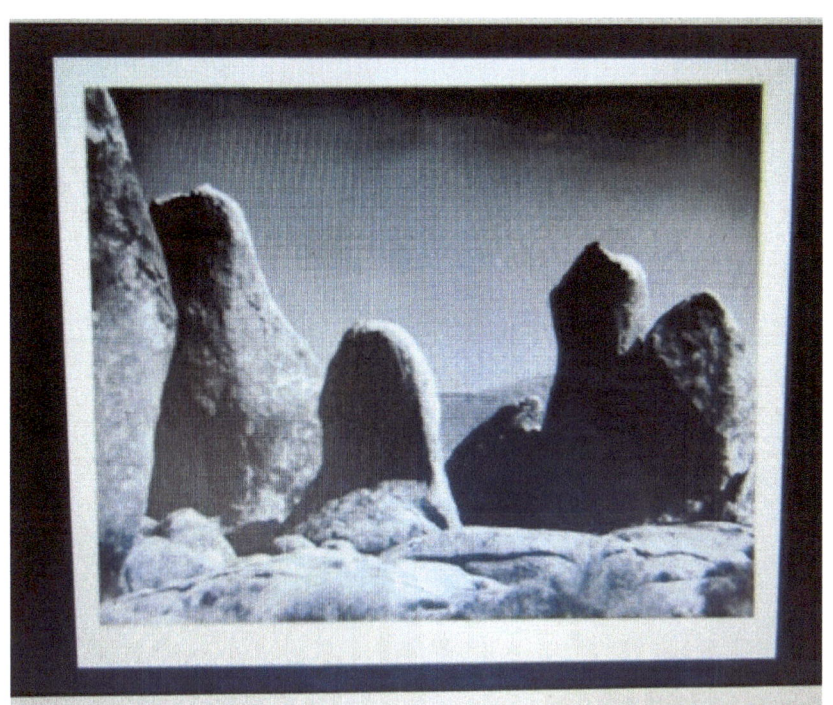

ALABAMA HILLS BY DOLPH. Photograph.

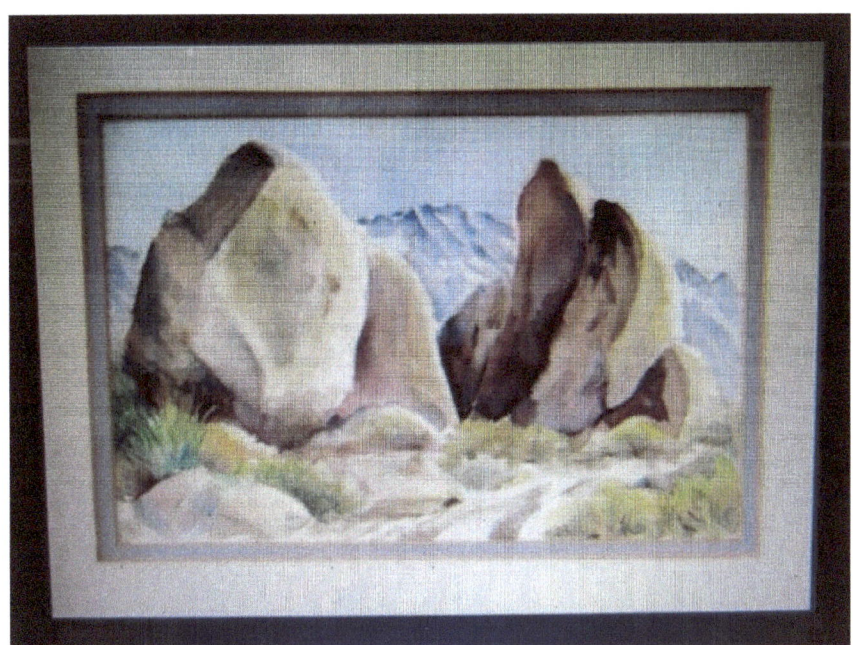

ALABAMA HILLS BY RUTH. Watercolor.

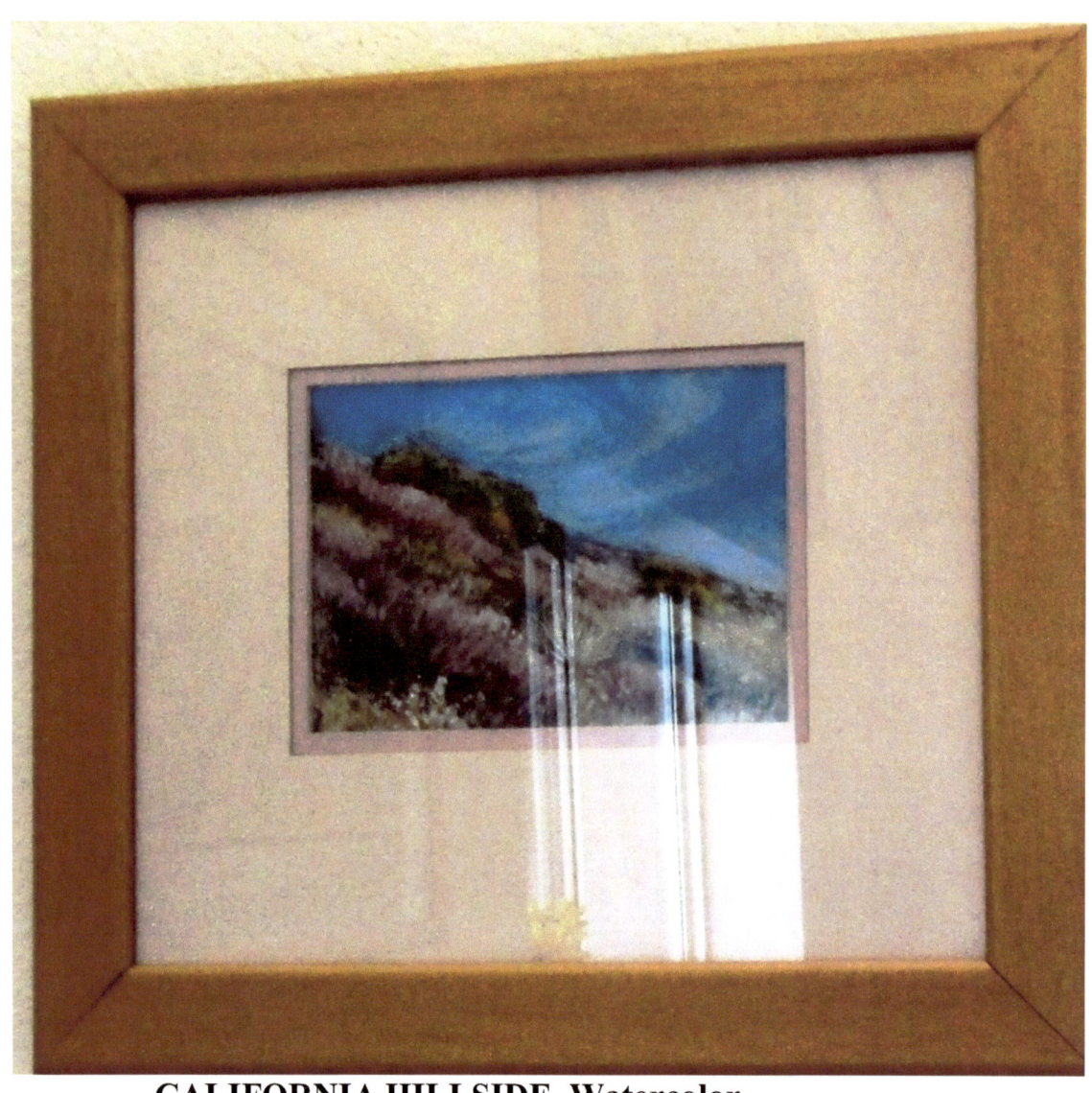

CALIFORNIA HILLSIDE. Watercolor.
We parked by the side of the road and saw this scene up the hill.

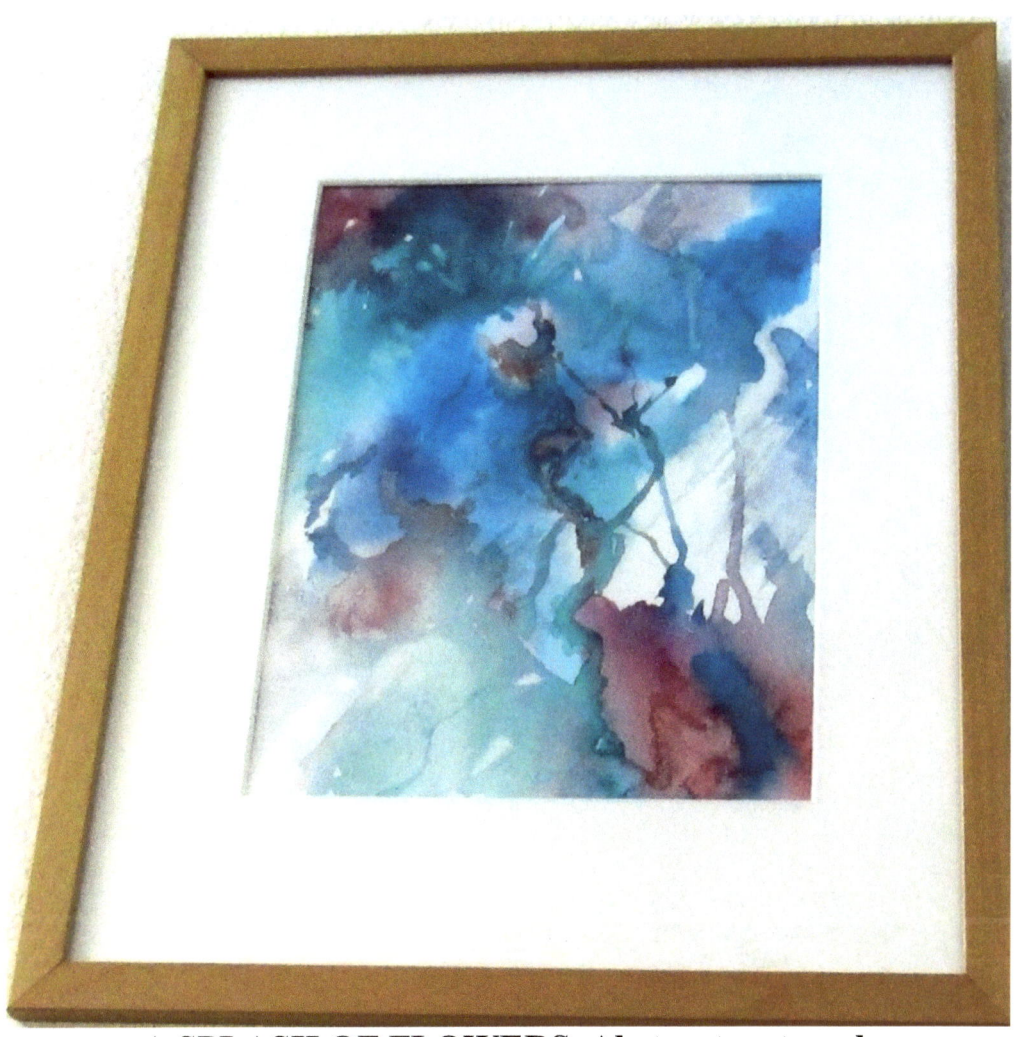

A SPLASH OF FLOWERS. Abstract watercolor.
    This was done by splashing paint and tipping the paper to form lines. They looked like flowers, and I left some white spaces to emphasize the shapes.

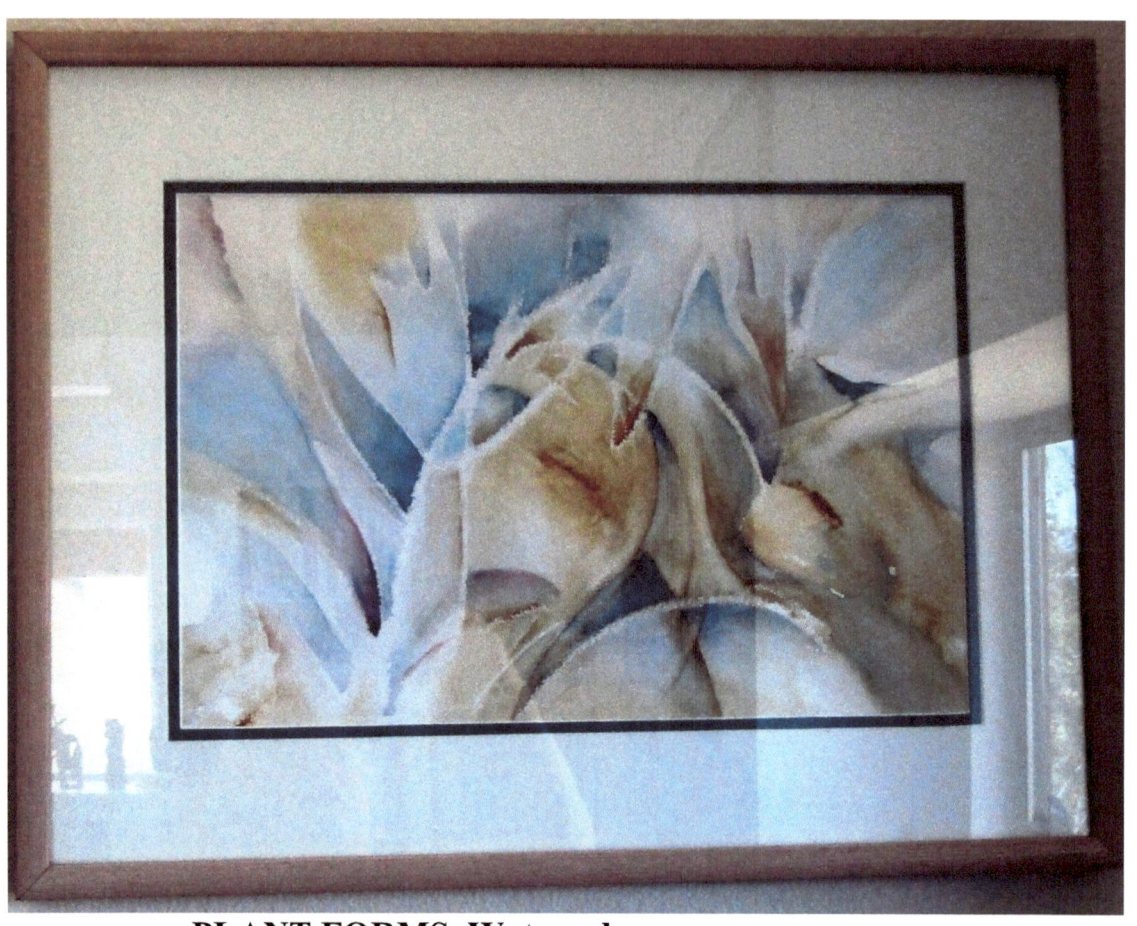

PLANT FORMS. Watercolor.
    I used a candle to draw lines to form shapes and which gave them depth and dimension. It is a resist technique. The paint will not stick to the wax.

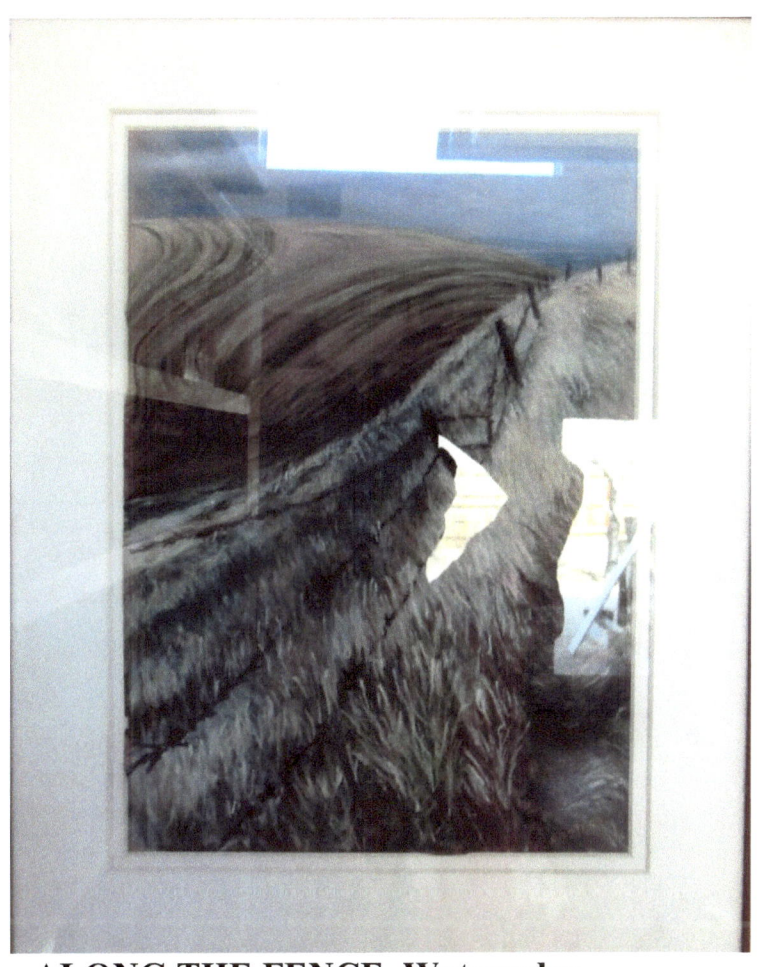

ALONG THE FENCE. Watercolor.
The fence shape divided the land into the plowed hill and the natural grass.

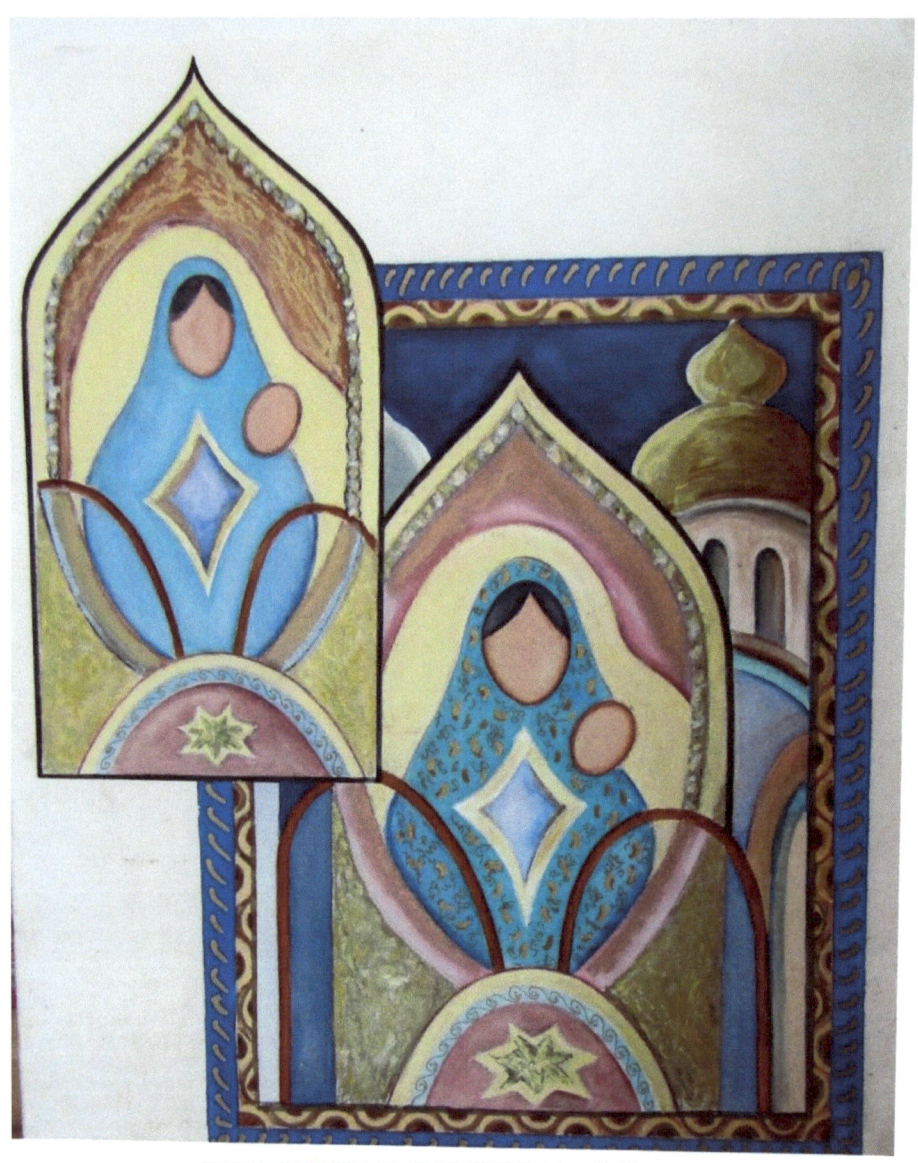

OUR TRIP TO RUSSIA. Oil.

Dolph and I took a wonderful trip to Russia. This painting is inspired by those wooden dolls that stack one inside the other. A Russian church is in the background of the stylized Madonna and Child.

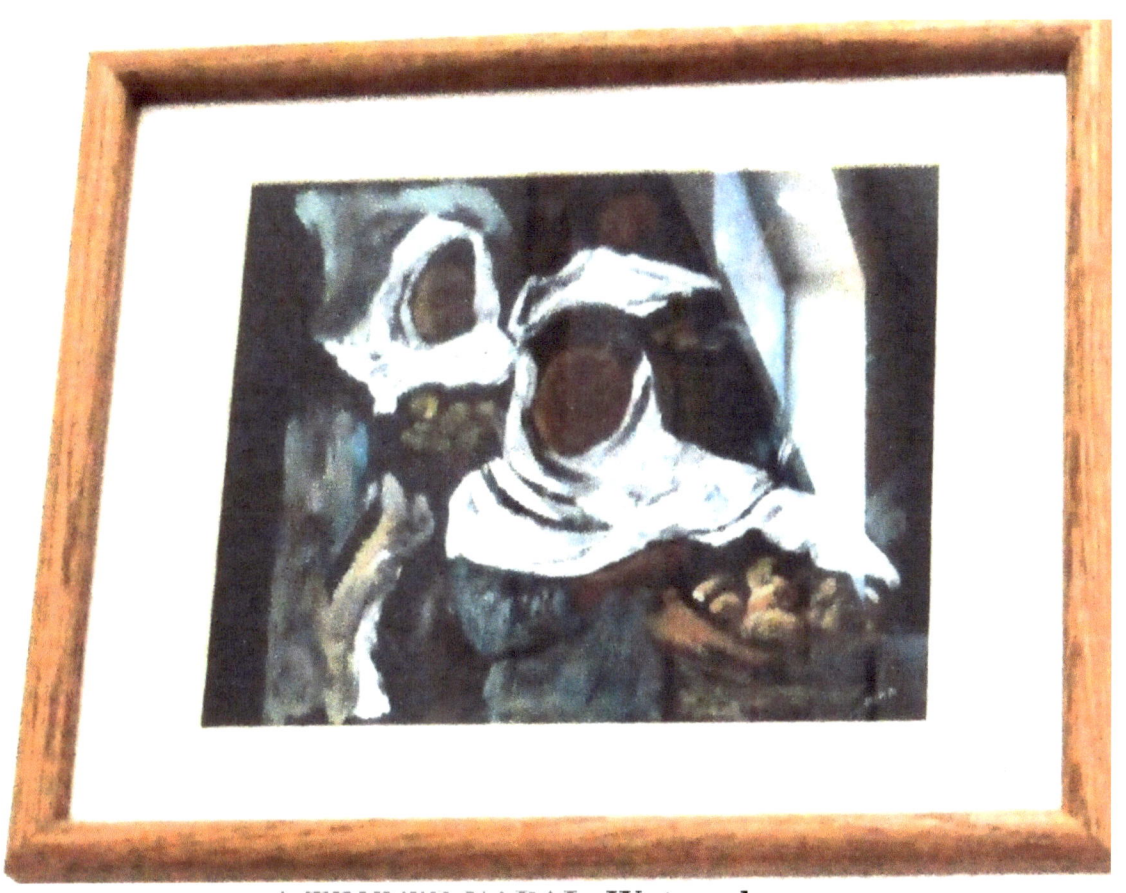

A TRIP TO NAPAL. Watercolor.
One of our travels. Children lined up outside the train to sell their goodies.

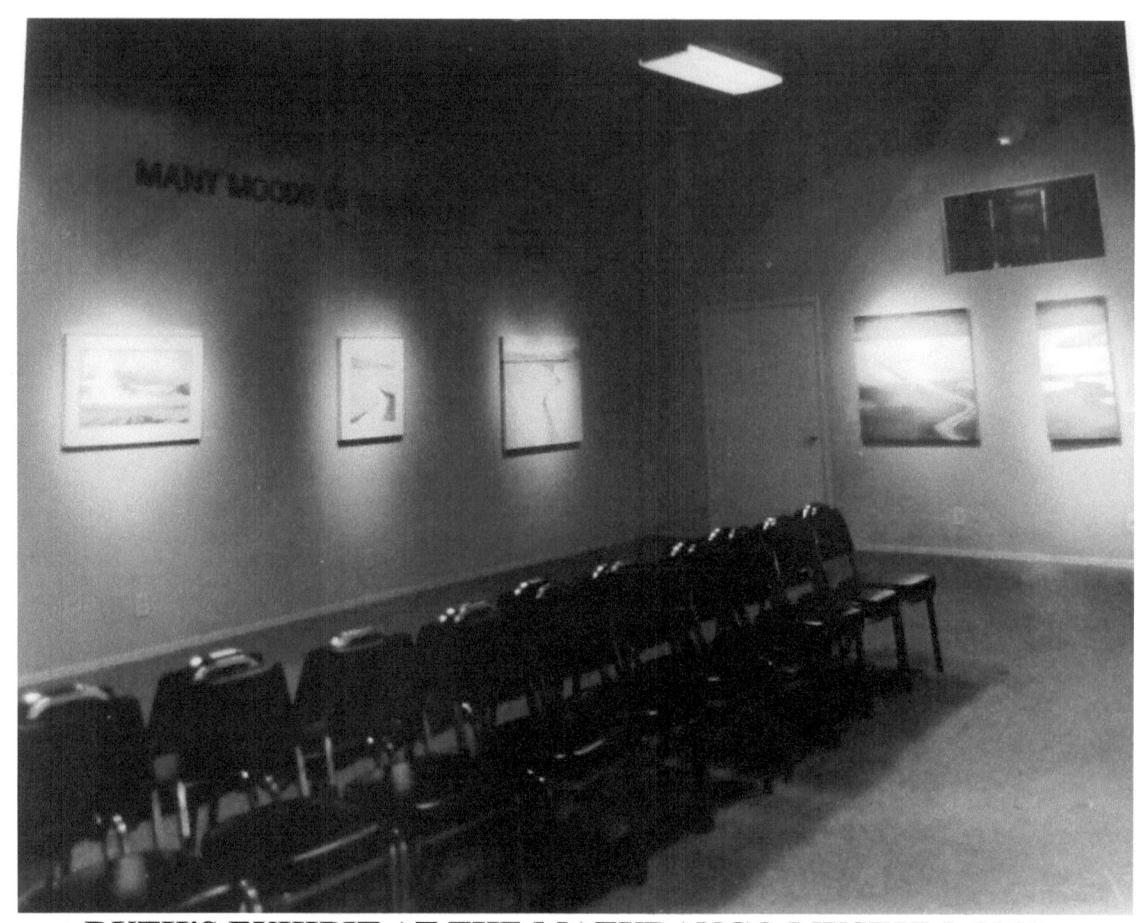
RUTH'S EXHIBIT AT THE MATURANGO MUSEUM, 2003.

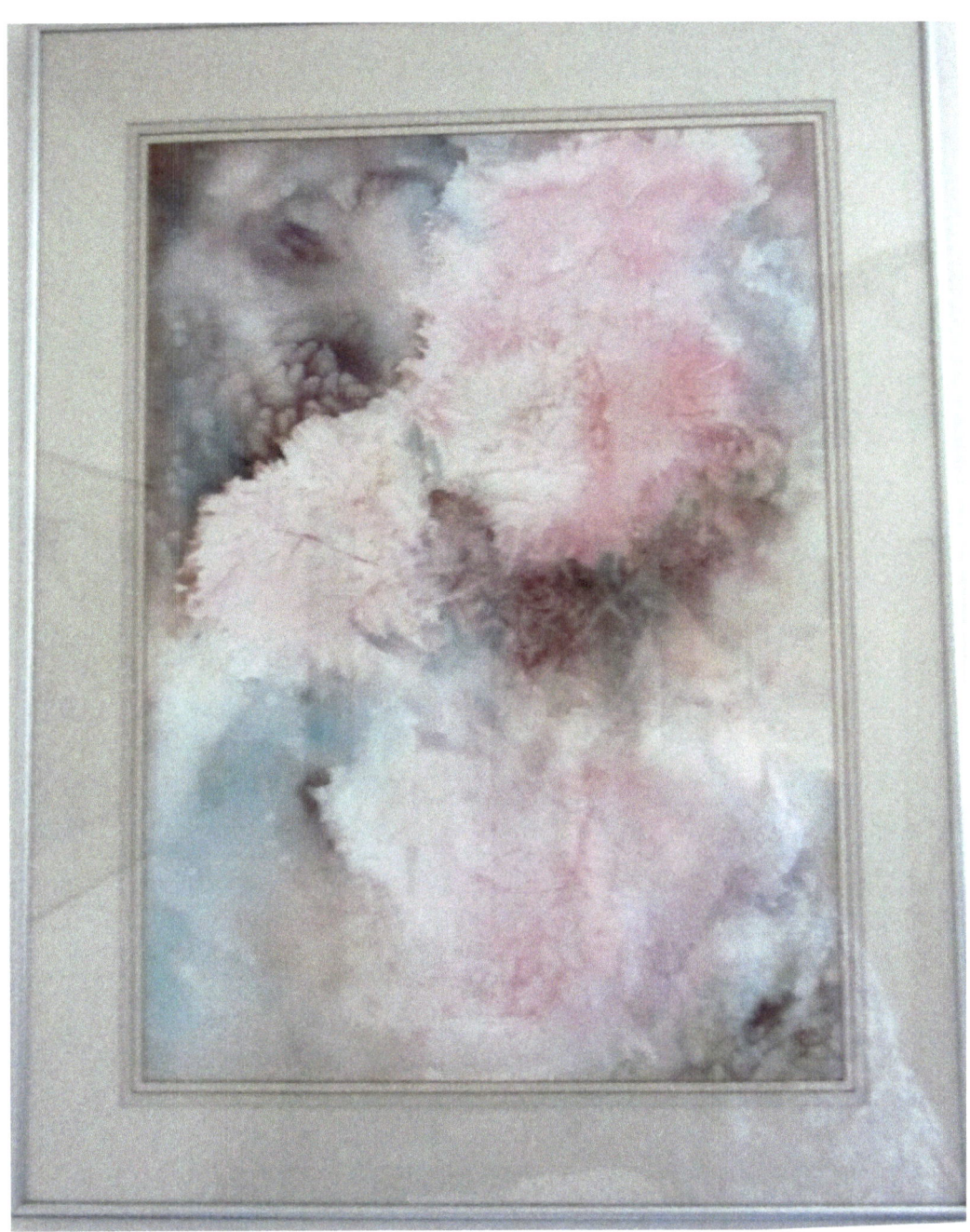

SMOKE TREE FLOWERS. Watercolor.
    A smoke tree in spring, with beautiful pink flowers. The first really large watercolor I attempted. I used a number of techniques. It also reminds me of those Italian ices on a stick.

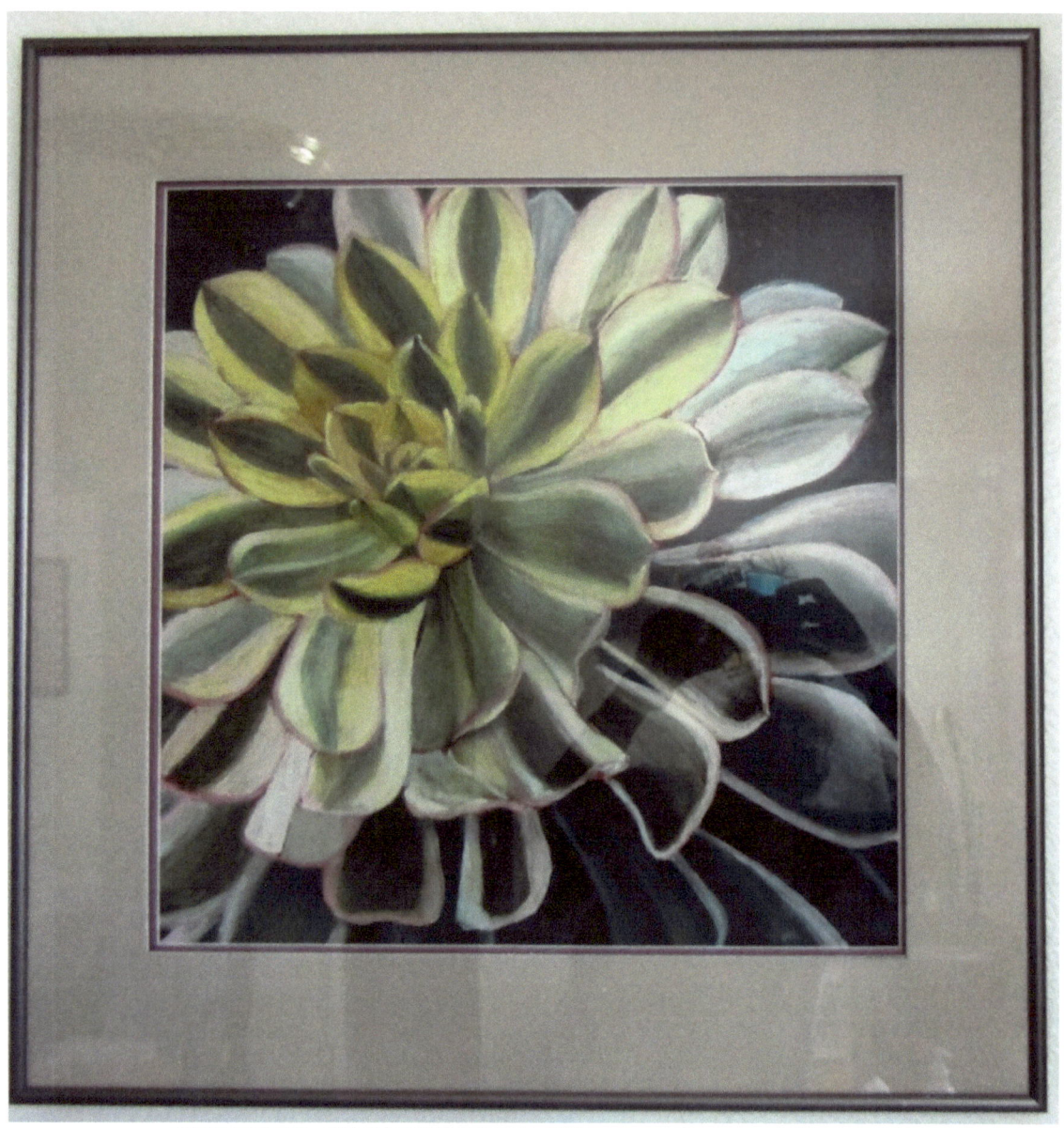

STRIPED SUCCULENT. Watercolor.
 The leaves form an abstract pattern. The green and white leaves add more contrast.

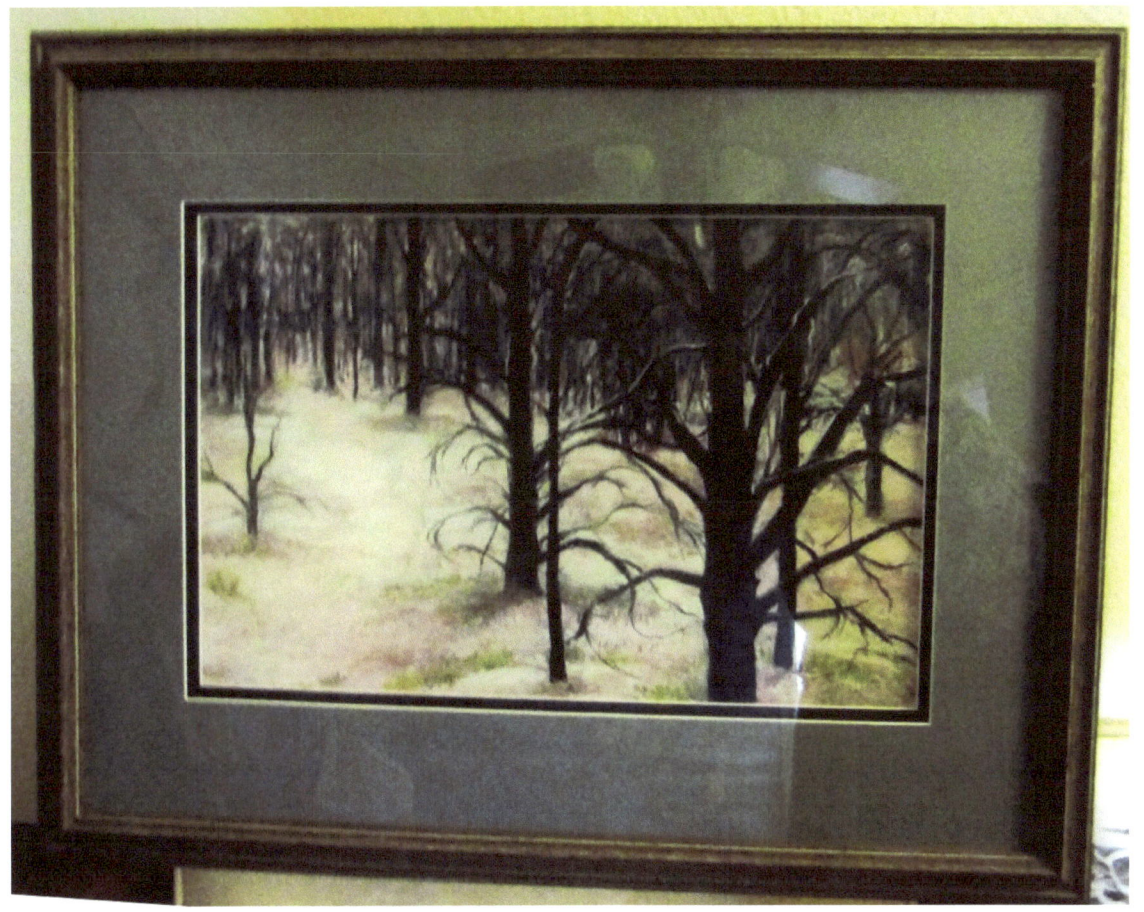

BURNED TREES. Watercolor.

There was a fire in Kennedy Meadows. This was early spring. Wild flowers of different colors were coming up and gave color to the ground. The trees looked like match sticks. They were skeletal. I enjoyed working on this. It is a challenge when you don't have too many hills in the background.

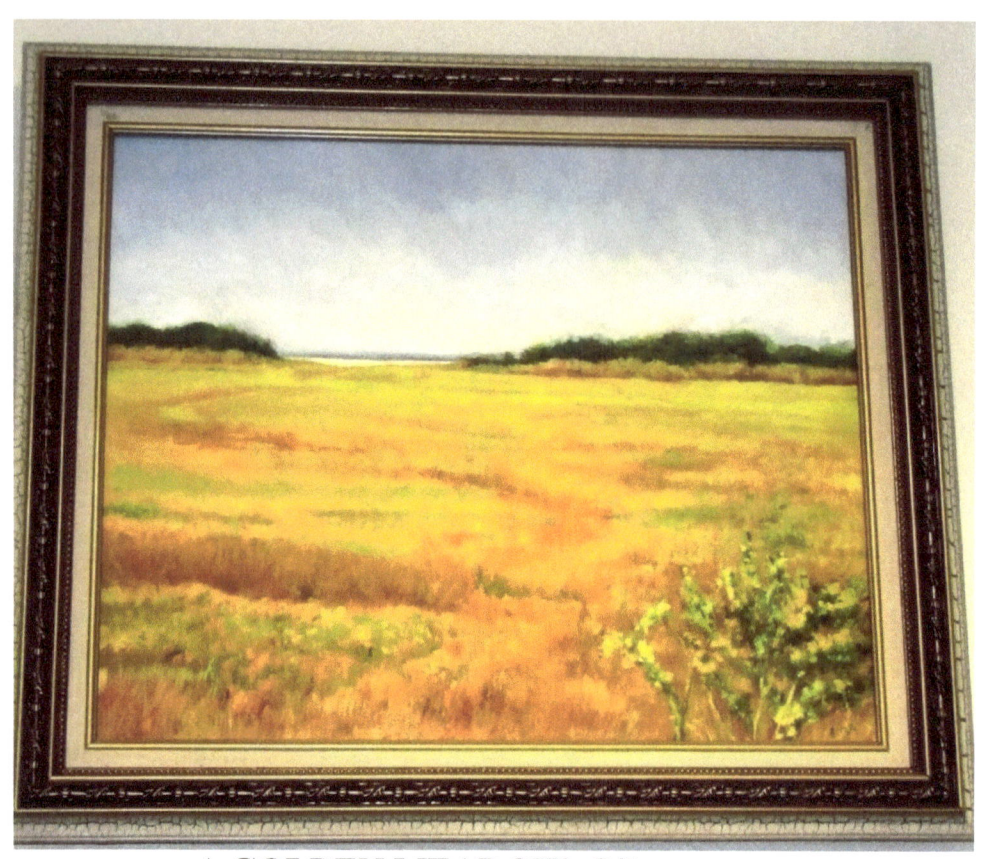

A GOLDEN MEADOW. Oil.
A meadow on the way to Monterey.

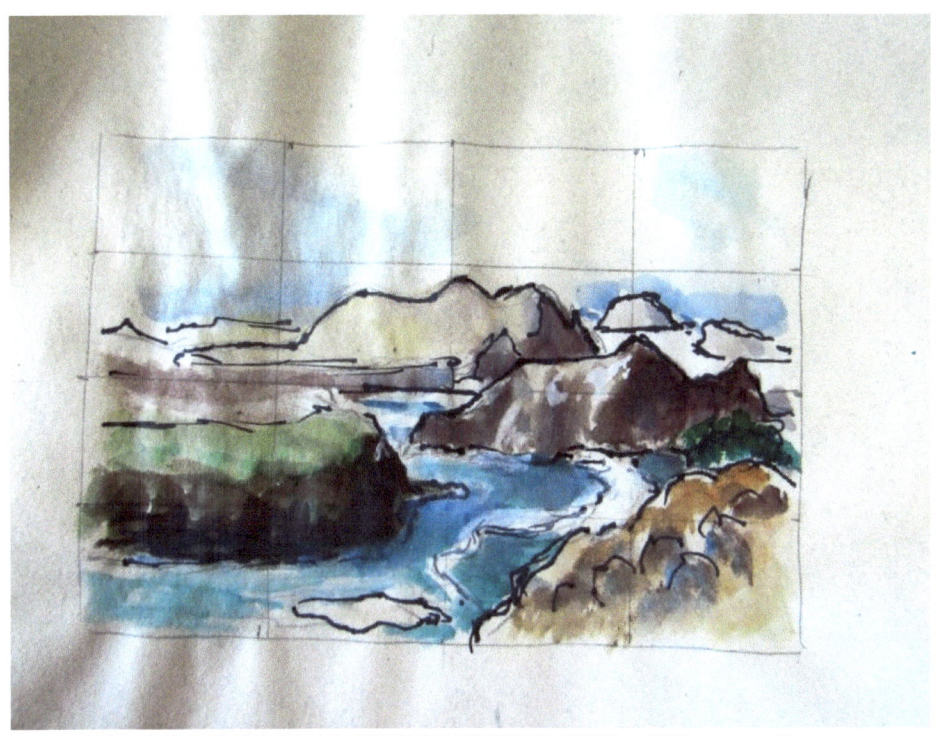

FROM RUTH'S SKETCHBOOK.   Watercolor.
A river flowing to the ocean near Monterey.

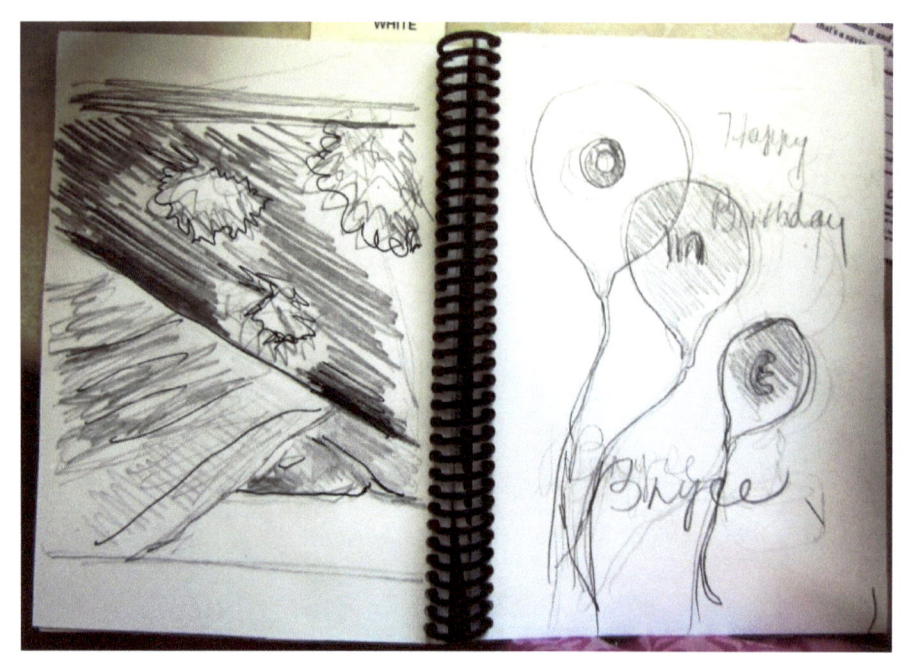

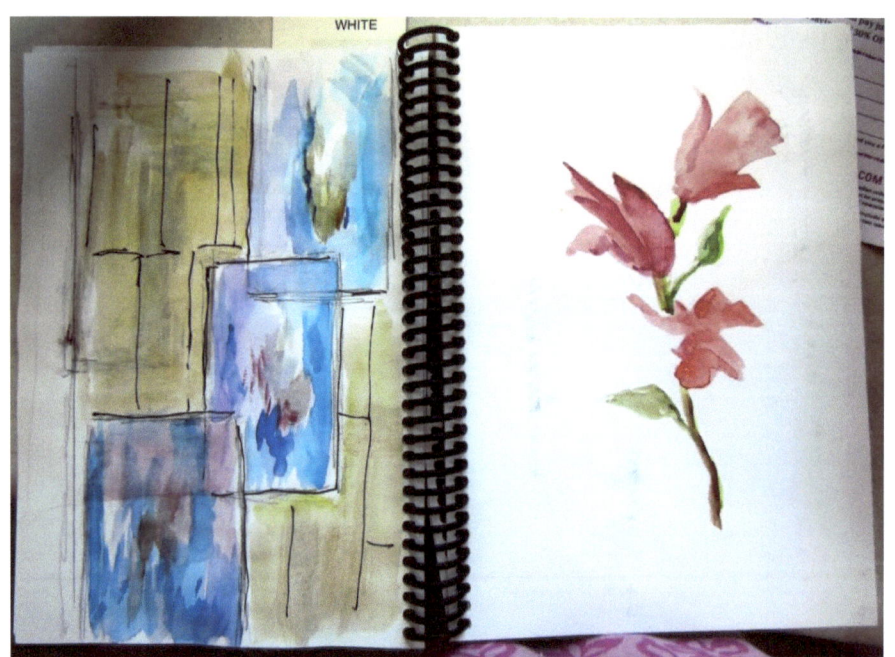

RUTH'S SKETCH BOOK.

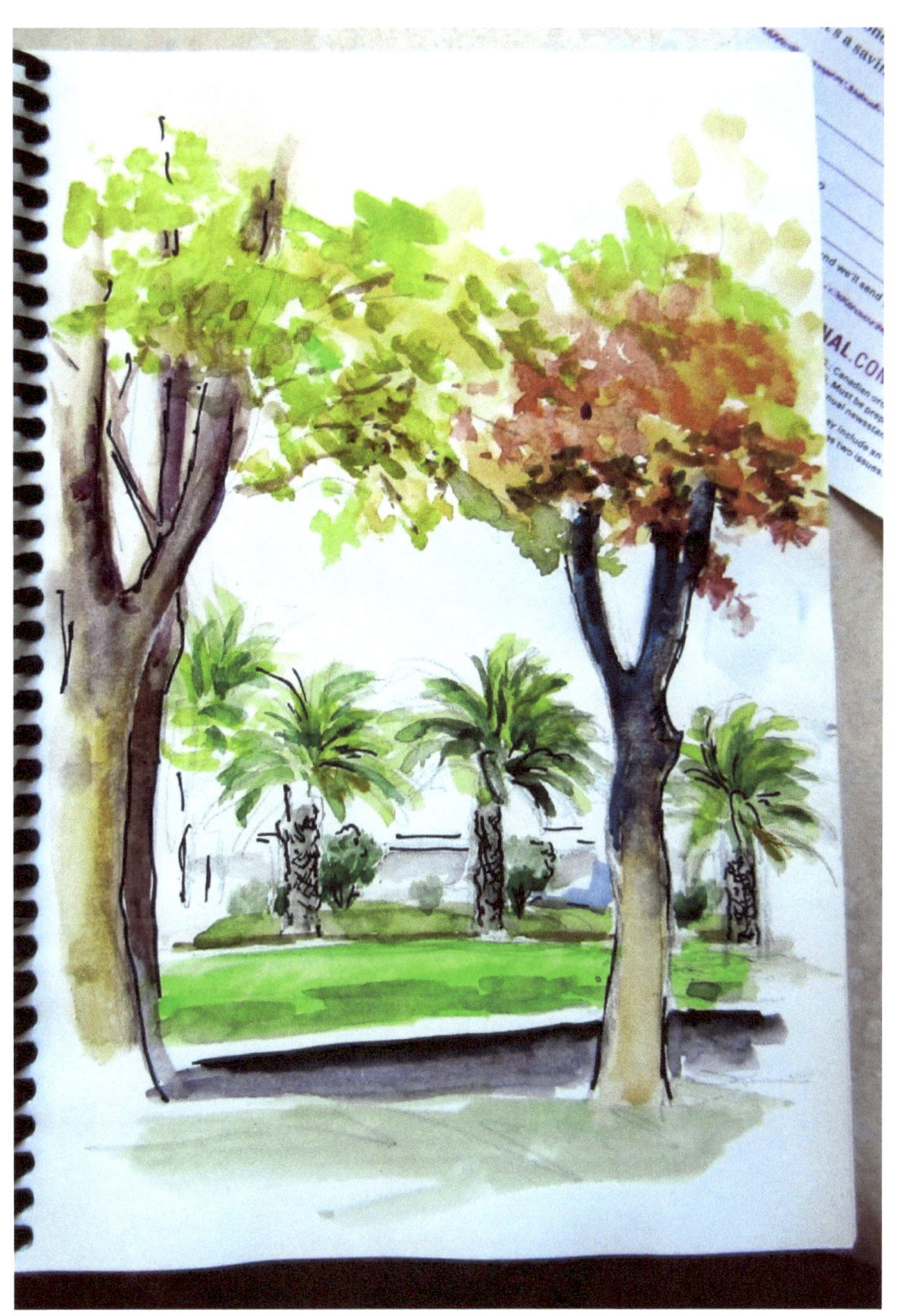
RUTH'S SCETCH OF TREES IN A PARK. Watercolor.

DOLPH'S PHOTO OF THE CENTURY PLANT.

It's interesting to see how he tackled the subject and how I did it. That is my husband's picture of an agave or century plant. It's very design oriented. The emphasis isn't what kind of a plant it is. We know that it is a plant. It's the pattern that makes it so interesting.

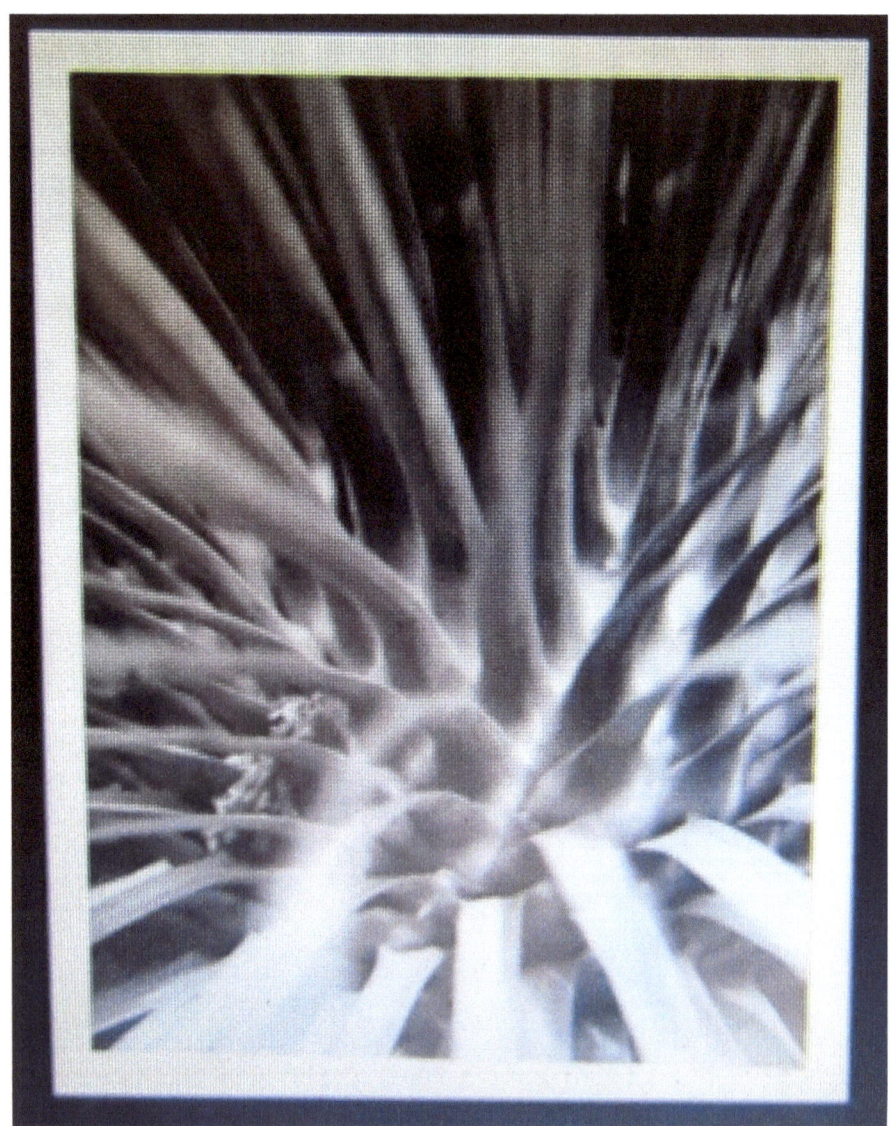

DOLPH'S PHOTO OF THE CENTURY PLANT

RUTH'S CENTURY PLANT.

When I wanted to do that, I saw something very different. I didn't see as much of a pattern. I saw those thorns. They fascinated me. That's how that plant affected me. I saw the shapes. It was quite sculptural. My interpretation is an emphasis on those thorns rather than the cactus spread out into a pattern. There's a big difference. For some reason or another, my painting looks ominous. I was thinking of the thorns. I think I captured that. Where Dolph didn't see it as a flower or a plant. I think he saw a very interesting pattern of shapes.

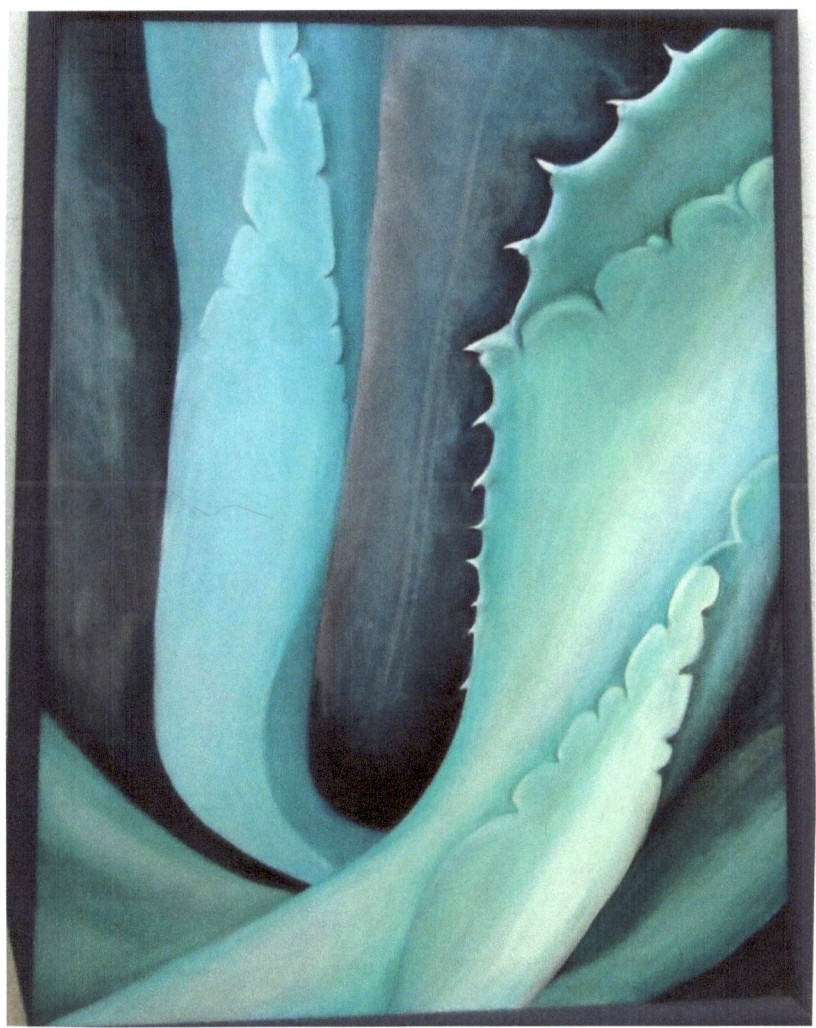

RUTH'S CENTURY PLANT.

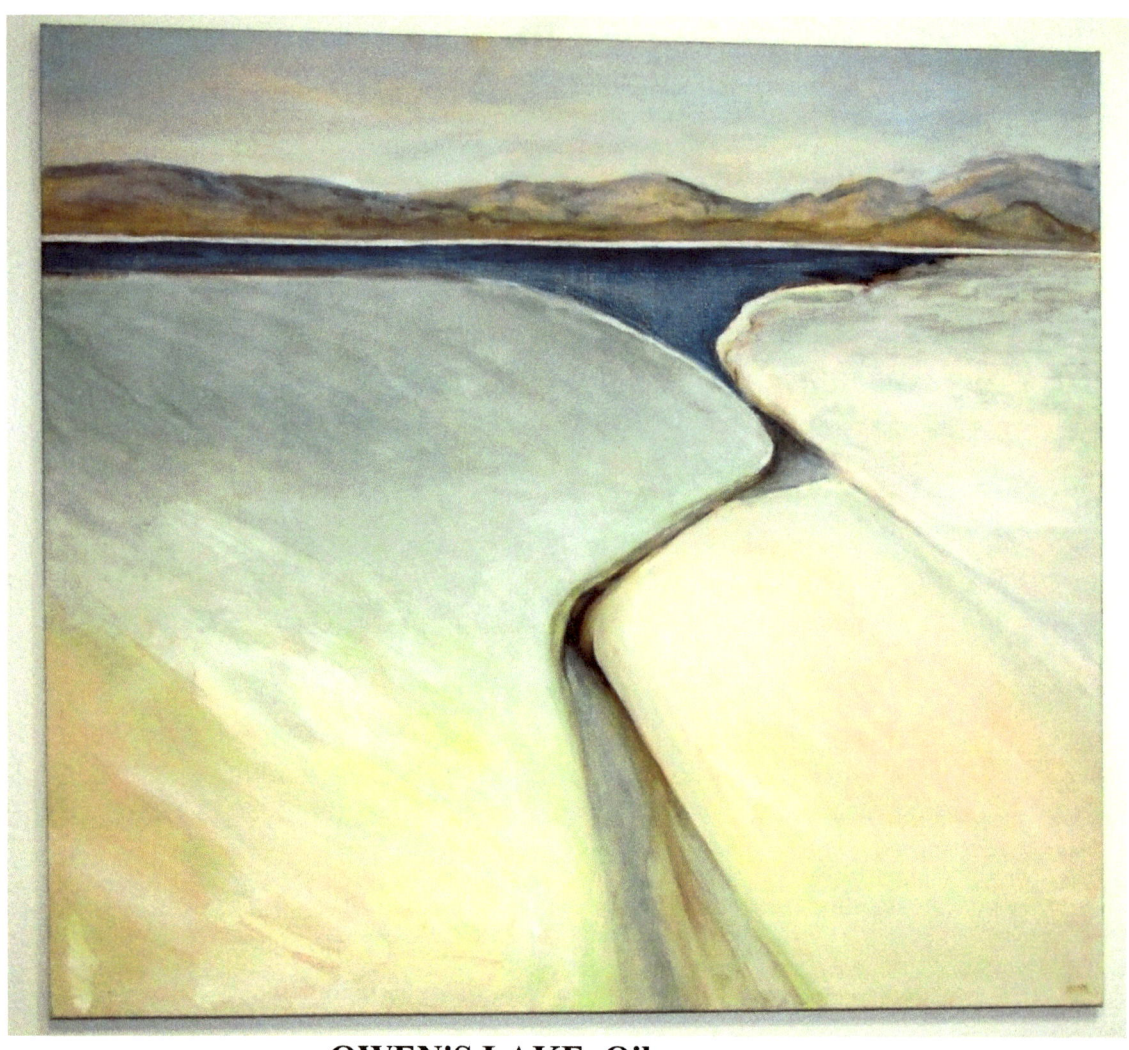

OWEN'S LAKE. Oil.

I was taken by the shapes and simple forms created by the sand shores of the lake.

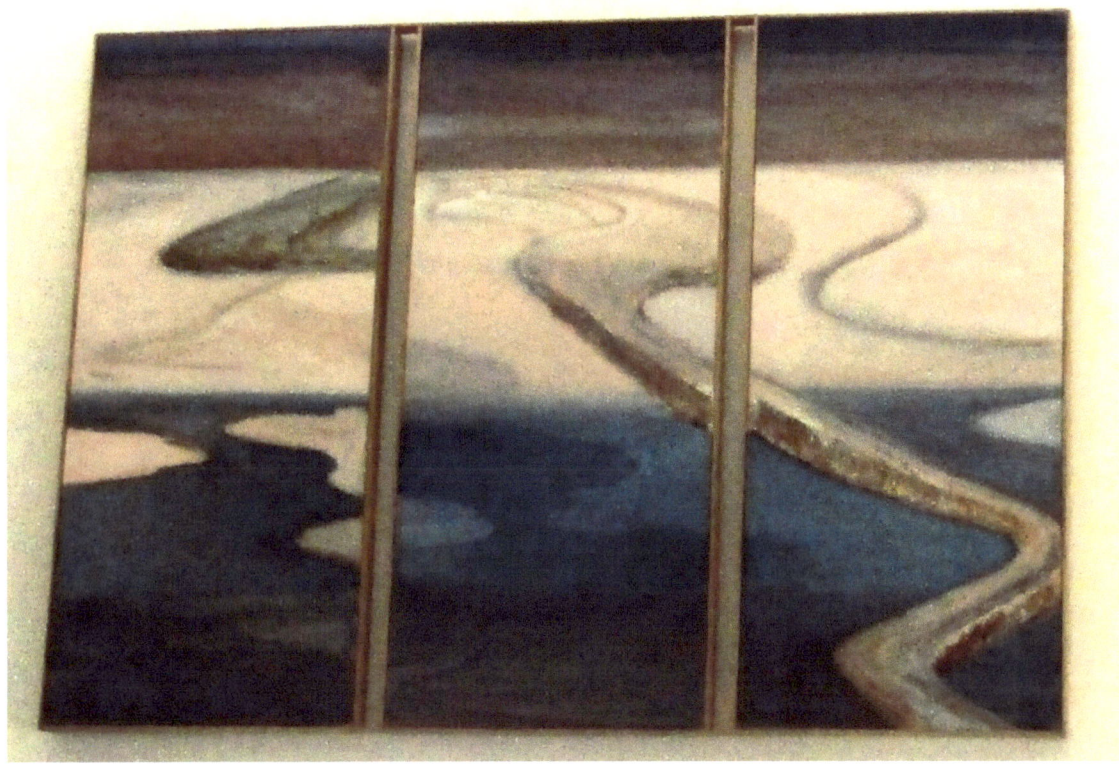
OWEN'S LAKE TRIPTYCH. Oil.

This is the opposite view, showing the water in the foreground with streams flowing toward the mountains.

FEELINGS.

The word that sums up Ruth Amster's art is "Feelings." She sees a scene or an object and it gives her a feeling that she wants to capture and convey to the viewer. Some of her work is realistic but there is an abstract quality of design that make each painting unique.

Ruth has a sense of humor, is kind, and is well liked by her many friends. She has one son, Ken, who also lives in Ridgecrest, California.

Vivian Chepourkoff Hayes

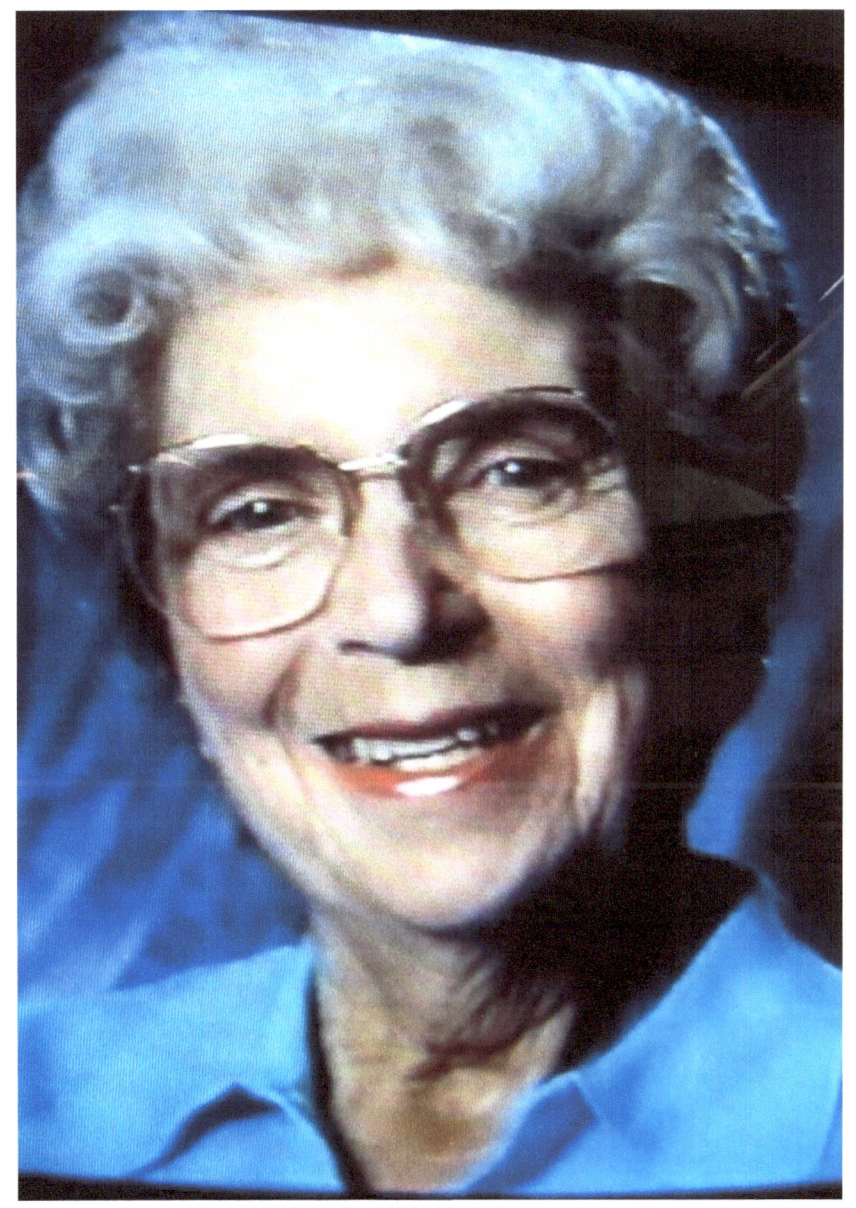

RUTH AMSTER.

www.ingramcontent.com/pod-product-compliance
Lightning Source LLC
Chambersburg PA
CBHW040411220526
45473CB00004B/1208